The WOBBAQUAS

Millennials Warriors

By

Wilma Sheltman

ISBN: 978-1-962224-80-2

Dedication

I dedicate this book to my Great-grandchildren. The ones who shine like a foreign star in the northern sky.

The motivation of my heart to write of adventure, love, excitement, and graven images.

Writing words and phrases that will enlighten people who take the time to read.

My family who is the burning torch in my life, I dedicate this book to you for years to come.

Acknowledgement

Loving children as she does her work as a writer represents them. Wilma helped raise some of her grandchildren. Reminiscing about the late-night stories she told of ship captains and made-up characters.

Motivated by her wonderful family, those who encourage and openly brag about her accomplishments. The team players who make up this wonderful family. She visits her computer daily to rehash the made-up tale from the night before she structures a story.

The love of children will make one delve inside to pull out a character to throw on his demeanor. Snuggled down in the bed, her grandsons await the nightly story Wilma comes up with. Her love for them shows what a wonderful life she expects for them. Motivated by what she reads, she twists the tale to make them get still. Slumber comes to these three wonderful grandchildren, and she flips off the light. May this book enrich your life while encouraging the writer to continue writing.

About the Author

Wilma Sheltman worked through her life only to semi-retire and write books. Working in her community Church all her life, she raised her grandchildren and great-grandchildren. Wilma is a loving woman with plenty of love to share. She shares some whimsical knowledge that only comes from the grid of life. Wilma's writing is not solely for entertainment; she hopes these tidbits of wisdom will resonate with her readers and give them a deeper understanding of the human experience.

With her remarkable imagination as her greatest gift, she crafts stories that intertwine the old and the new, infusing them with her creativity. Wilma believes that if anyone slows down and wants to immerse in a quiet moment, they should soak up some quiet time with a good book.

Thank you for coming into my imaginary world.

Millennial Warriors

Overview

In 2020, the sands are still hot off the coast of Africa. The galactic alien space travelers inside their spaceships look magnificent and phantasmic. They have arrived to seed two modules in Earth's oceanic waters.

More than 2,000 years ago, spaceships arrived, designed to explore distant planets. Within these vessels were ancient aliens serving as space travelers. Navigating the ships were '*Paranites*', fellow space explorers. These galactic entities journeyed through space centuries earlier to spread life on various planets, including Earth. Their presence left a lasting impact on civilization, evident in ancient runways across the upper plateau grounds. Hieroglyphics inside the spaceships and scattered across Egypt's dusty mountain plains today further validate their visit. Abandoned tombs of kings and queens hold pyramid-shaped artifacts strewn across the hot desert surface. Indeed, predetermined space travelers arrived in a remarkable formation tasked with seeding supernatural beings. These beings had no place in the universe except on a planet with a suitable atmosphere to nurture the contents of their pods. Earth became their chosen home, intended for them to flourish and evolve into a thriving civilization named after their celestial origins.

Originating from their ancestral lineage on the Wobbaquas' home planet, situated millions of light-years away in the vast expanse of space, they inherited the name Wobbaquas due to their distinctive gait. The earth that gave them life is a vast aquatic realm characterized by abundant water—hence the amalgamation of "Wob" and "aqua." Over centuries, progressing as a society, their development has been extraordinary. Nurtured within the depths of the ocean's deepest crevices on planet

Earth, they have mastered the manipulation of seawater, becoming adept water benders and aquatic beings. Believing in a higher power and knowing the master of the universe has become an inner-born characteristic.

SONG
The Warriors

Sparkling like blue lightning,
The warriors of the blue hue,
The millennials of deep, the fighter's true,
Guarding the gate of the depths, a crew,
The fighters, the aquifers, resemble two.

Guarding the gate of the masters.
The fighters, those are keeping the deep truth,
Managing a kingdom, keeping the space blue.

The warriors, the aquifers of the sea,
Armed, ready at the slightest sign,
The warriors unending,
The protectors, the servers,
Of the united aquatic kingdom.

The warriors, the aquifers of the blue,
The sparkle of their armor shining through.
The guardians of the deep serve you,
These breeds uphold the deep,
Never to be underestimated by all warriors, indeed.
The aquifers are complete.
The warrior's aquifers of the sea

Warriors of the deep

Longevity

We found some pottery jugs at the trench in the sea,
The jugs looked corroded with plankton from years in water you see,
We suspect one of these holds the secret to longevity.

A secret sent by a queen to another continent, a treasure for a king,
We could lose the mystical jug among these,
The color of longevity will appear to shine in the sea,
I watch for a flicker of color while looking upon these,
maybe as luck will have it, for me.

The jugs prepared by the aquifers of the sea for a queen, maybe,
Longevity in one,
a treasure the pirated, who sink ships, a treasure in some,
A gift to the ocean should one go adrift or see these,
A treasure for the finder among this Longevity,
the treasure of the salty sea, adrift.
They lost this precious gift at sea,
by an overturned ship,
one whipped by the windy sea.
A finding in today's time,
one we cherish when uncovering artifacts,
in the depths sublime,
Piercing the depths of a crew in our time.

CHARACTERS

Millennial Man - An astute leader of an underwater world with a slim stature and a loving spirit. A loner, one who depends on no one. Millennial man leads with full authority! He was a magical man determined to spend his life protecting and honoring the Wobbaquas. Those that make up his aquatic world in the depths of the ocean.

Orbital Man- Second to his counterpart in the aquatic world of the Wobbaquas. A feminine demeanor, a brother, a friend, an aquifer, a lover of water, one who helps and never like a thorn in their side in his world.

Orbital Man – The purpose in his life is to take care of the father, a magical man, a transparent spirit, keeper of the gate. Orbital is a meek recluse, a shy person, and a loner who speaks from an isolated spot. Many cried out at him for his clothing and found that droop. Sheltered by his brother, he is such an intelligent Wobbaqua. He adds luster to the underwater world. Orbital.

The Father - An unseen spirit, he is invisible and only comes to his own. As quickly as the sparkle in the water appears, so too does the father. Invisible, he can be heard only as a voice, yet able to move mountains. A magical one and keeper of the gate, he is the protector of all the gatekeepers of the underworld. He comes from the chariot of Wobbaqua, a life of the galactic seawater world, inside the temple wall. Only for his brother, the Millennial man, and his counterpart, the Orbital man, to see.

Brick Thunder- Magnificent young man, tall, slim, human with a muscular physique, handsome, energetic, the style of the times, shaven head and beard. The demeanor of a knowledgeable man, leadership abilities, a master marksman, a sword thrower, bravery unmatched with a keen eye like a hawk, a peacekeeper, lover, and loner. Investigator, public servant, and intellectual, he is good at changing his identity by changing his apparel.

Marlina- She is a woman of tall stature, beautiful human, dark-completed, loving spirit, dark eyes, long fingers, and the shape of a mermaid, caring and kind, coming from Spanish descent. A streak of lean as a woman, she is a bright, capable intellectual individual with her own story. Her beauty and good humor capture people's attention—she is a vibrant and beautiful woman. A lonely woman, abandoned by her true love, lost at sea.

Old Spud- Boisterous Wobbaqua is an old Fisherman who can make anything work mechanically. His abilities were evident only when something needed redesigning. Designed from ivory, he shaves it down to fit the shape of his teeth. Carrying it in his sleeve of scales, he has access to it at all times; he even uses it to unlock doors. Spuds can roll into a ball when sleeping. Spud is a skinny, older man-shaped Wobbaqua.

Contents

Dedication iii

Acknowledgement iv

About the Author v

Overview vii

SONG The Warriors ix

Longevity xi

CHARACTERS xii

Chapter One 1

Evolution Of the Wobbaquas 1

Chapter Two 16

Where They Went? 16

Chapter Three 23

Crime Rates Rise to reach New York 23

Chapter Four 29

Aquatic Weapons 29

Chapter Five 56

Breeding 56

Chapter Six 67

Falling in Love 67

Chapter Seven 80

Heart-Wrenching 80

Chapter Eight 100

The War of Both Worlds 100

Chapter Nine 121

The Temple 121

Chapter Ten 130

Ol' FisherMan: The Battle 130

Chapter Eleven 135
War Beside the City 135
Chapter Twelve 143
The War in the Abyss 143
Chapter Thirteen..155
Casualties 155
Chapter Fourteen 160
Their Need to Rebuild..160
Chapter Fifteen..163
Closing Back into The Deep 163
Chapter Sixteen 170
Return to the Depths..170
Chapter Seventeen..176
The Proposal..176
Chapter Eighteen..182
The City Awaits Its Queen..182
Chapter Nineteen..186
The Wedding Day..186
Chapter Twenty..190
The Ceremony 190

Chapter One

Evolution Of the Wobbaquas

Several astronomical changes occur within the majestic galaxy around Earth. In the past, alien space travelers left Earth years before, leaving traceable landing pads in Egypt. Many are within the areas around the hot sand of the desert and majestic pyramids in the vast sandy plains of Africa. Those that remain, playing their part in the Universe, checking back on seeded planets, space travelers travel the star-laden crevices of deep space. As custodians of good, as their mission on this planet is complete, they seamlessly blend into their surroundings. Their alien spacecraft gracefully glides across the nocturnal sky, appearing as a mere streak of light to the unaided eye. Blending into its surroundings, the alien spacecraft veers across the night sky, seen as only a streak of light to the naked eye. Two pods of seedlings from other planets are onboard to seed Earth's oceans. Strapped to the gray inner-lined shell of the magnificently structured spacecraft, they were more advanced than earthly vessels. Space ships so advanced it's unimaginable, and their ability to enter atmospheres untouched. The advanced spaceships are the same as a city as humans know it. For example, the Nubian Aquifer in Africa is circling for the exact placement of the drop; this is one of the world's largest underground sources of fresh water. Since they run under the pyramids, they are a source of fresh water for aquifers who live and flourish inside them.

The seed pods have to thrive in the content of seawater. Being eighty percent H20, Earth has become the prime place for this phenomenal task. They are navigating toward the astronomical runways on the desert sand. Many hoovering across the sky, silent, unnoticed, and invisible as a sparkling light, landing upon the tallest mountainside. On the high mountains of the African continent, beside the edge of the Sea of Galilee, the sun opens the hatch on the spaceship. All the occupants become invisible to the naked eye of humans, including the ship. Once the hatch opens, they step into existence and begin to materialize instantly, a fully dressed procession of royalty in space travelers emerging once outside the ship, fully clad in grandeur and having apparatuses to protect them from germs entering the spaceship. A veil of sparkling nothing surrounds each one, preventing anything from coming upon them. Assembled outside the ship are workers—those who make this procession move.

Rising the ship atop a distant pyramid, each worker is in a loincloth, non-male or female, just smooth bodies. Each has a sparkle around them for protection, and each soldier of the space epic seeding crew.

Leaving the ship at sunrise, they throw down their hands with open palms up; this is the same as a salute to others. Suddenly, a superb carpet appeared, opening in mid-air, and they placed the seed pod cocoons on the carpet. Prepared, they have the two pods upon a magic carpet precisely as the star travelers specified. Aliens walk upright beside the carpet to make the delivery. Orders are to 'Make a precise placement of these two gray-green metallic pods. Both cocoons are to be seeded in this planet's oceanic waters.

The beginning of a new world of Wobbaquas!

They walked down the pyramid steps, looked around, left the spacecraft at the top, and focused on the job. The procession stops at the edge of the sea. The magic carpet floats to the ground just above the surface, mystically raised to a higher elevation, telepathically from their place on the red and blue translucent carpet. When the carpet shadows the sand beneath it, the sand becomes smooth for the aliens to step softly upon—floating slowly to the clear water's edge. They are released into open water from a hovering carpet.

Two babies from another world nestled comfortably inside their birthing cocoon. Each cylinder descends beneath the clear, pristine water's surface, alien pods intertwined by their souls and two babies of the same seedling mother pod. Both thrive inside two cocoons to produce civilization and time charts pace time. These charts were in the Valley of the Kings in Egypt and were well defined; the millennials have them within their time frame in the hereafter. Minute lines show the coming of sun rays that shine beneath the abyss. Rainbow in the depths. Rainbows have several units stretched from one area of the sea to the other. Warriors have time in their minds.

Every individual possesses an innate internal clock, a guide that signals the passage of time, a unique occurrence known as Wobbaqua. This mental programming commences when a baby Wobbaqua becomes intertwined with a jellyfish. Each mermaid who nourishes and fosters a baby knows what needs to be done when following the pre-determination of their fate by the masters of the Universe. Submerged beneath the water's surface, the cocoons bask in the morning sunlight, commencing incubation. The ticking sound confirms life's emergence within the cocoon, a signal the alien beings perceive before they retreat to their spaceship. Swiftly ascending with a whirlwind of motion, they reach the pinnacle of the pyramid inside the vessel, vanishing into the vast expanse of space at the speed of light. A predetermined departure schedule binds these spacefaring warriors. Within a few hours of the seawater, they permeate the outer shell of the podded structure. Akin to dissolving the capsule's exterior, the baby's body gradually unfolds, resembling the flower's unfolding petals. Meanwhile, the babies emit a ticking sound, resonating from their soul spot—the essence of a Wobbaqua baby's soul.

“Yes! “This is the beginning of the Wobbaqua civilization!” Slowly, they are growing into what they will become. The birth process appears slowly, the nurturing brown, slow-moving. Sea otters come to wait. The sea otters come to rescue the ticking noise. They were leaving her siblings beside the seashore line.

Gracefully, she submerges herself beneath the translucent, pristine seawater with its captivating aqua hue. Her quest is to uncover the source of the sound. As she searches, the cylinder rupture elicits the curious gaze of a sea otter nearby. Two babies emerge from these space-worthy cylinders, their large eyes and adorned fins marking their extraterrestrial origins. They crack open at the tranquil water's edge, revealing their mechanical shells. One of these seemingly insignificant creatures inches its way toward the sea otter, instinctively seeking nourishment and knowledge. Embracing the bountiful surroundings, the sea otter mother with a newborn calf prepares to offer her milk to these extraordinary infants. It is a testament to the nurturing nature of sea otters, who extend their care beyond their offspring to welcome these unique arrivals.

Two cylinders unfold, unveiling humanoid figures whose skin possesses an uncanny resemblance to that of a fish, resembling the sleek fins of a trout. Their transformative skin transitions before one's eyes, initially glistening like human skin yet eventually manifesting scales akin to a fish's. Physically, both individuals possess identical portions of fins and strategically positioned gills, rendering them adept in aquatic environments. Carefully maneuvering towards the edge of the immaculate, white sandy beach, where palm trees bear witness to the whirl of hurricanes, these babies emit fewer sounds once submerged in water. With bodies shaped like humans, their presence on Earth finds purpose as their destiny unfolds—an eventual metamorphosis into submerged beings.

The otter observes, recognizing signs of life through their eyes and movements. One baby clings to the otter, seeking sustenance and paving the way for the other baby to access an alternate breast. Encircling the mother otter, akin to warm sand surrounding the pyramids, the babies experience the nurturing warmth of milk that sustains their existence. Innately driven to care for their offspring, otters never release their young ones alone into crystalline seawater. They nurture these remarkable infants alongside their offspring until they mature enough to transition to the care of the vibrant mermaids. Over time, these beautiful mermaids, adorned with a spectrum of colors like a rainbow, assume guardianship of these remarkable beings.

Growing up, they play in the seawater quietly, splash, and play away the day, leaving behind the sea otter. During the growing stage, up to ten human years before, they're released into seawater alone. Growing six and seven feet tall, Wobbaquas, through puberty, live off the jellyfish for knowledge until they mate and bring forth many offspring.

Time to wean them

Separated from the mermaids' nurturing breasts, they remain in their care until their fin cells develop, and they rely on the nutrients provided by the jellyfish cocoon. This essential process extends over several years, ensuring their survival in the merciless expanse of the oceanic waters they will forever call home. The designated ones have meticulously prepared them for this fate. The liberating moment arrives when puberty signals manifest, and the surrogate jellyfish intuitively knows to release them into the depths. With the emergence of small scales, they acquire the resilience to withstand the immense pressure within the ocean's caverns, albeit vulnerable in the tranquil, slow-moving currents of the depths.

As they reach the culmination of puberty, their bodies become adorned with an intricate pattern of tiny scales, symbolizing their readiness for release into the profound abyss. Many drift with the underwater currents, effortlessly accessing delectable sustenance, eliminating the need for arduous long-distance swims. The jellyfish that sheltered the young Wobbaquas succumb to the strain of nurturing them for an extended period, a predestined fate well understood from the outset. Upon entering the protective confines of the jelly sack, the young Wobbaquas connect to an umbilical cord, which attaches to their soul spot. Through this connection, they impart knowledge about the civilization that thrives in the deep-water world they are supposed to inhabit.

They reside indoors for several years, consuming lobster, as they possess the ability to undertake deep plunges following the attainment of puberty. Puberty for them occurs at ten years of age or older, measured in human years. As infants, mermaids nurture them until they reach an age suitable for nursing from the enormous jellyfish. "The stigma gigantic," a colossal guardian of the underworld, has only been sighted approximately 100 times in the past century. This titanic jellyfish has been observed in Japan and along the western coastline of North America. It is one of the largest predatory invertebrates in all oceans worldwide, except the Arctic. For millennia, the vast jellyfish's capabilities have been a part of their nurturing process.

Teen Wobbaquas lack scales, their translucent skin membrane allowing visibility inside the jellyfish, where they nurture until they reach ten years of age in human terms. Once they reach this milestone, each one is released into the depths of the sea as a mature Wobbaquas. They anchor themselves to the jellyfish's membrane using their soul spot. They are fed until they reach a humanoid-like form of a Wobbaqua. At this stage, they can see beyond the jellyfish and explore the depths to understand the life there. Once mature, the offspring join the community in Philippi, living among other Wobbaquas who have undergone the same transformation.

Many individuals train them, a process that takes place over the years after being positioned at the sea's edge in Galilee. Other Wobbaquas residing in the sea realm serve as mentors to teach them things that the jellyfish did not impart. This transition into adulthood holds significance for me.

They have heard tales of their ability to summon powerful storms that can sink ships. Yet, they are also regarded as wise instructors. Similar to mermaids, mermen possess the allure to captivate and entice humans. They possess enchanting beauty, emit soft and melodious tones, and hold a seductive aura as sirens who appreciate the enchanting qualities of singing voices. For many mermaiden species, migration is intertwined with the mating process. Wobbaquas, on the other hand, solely reproduce within their kind. While they share resemblances with fish and humans, their essence remains distinctly Wobbaqua, instilled in them since their upbringing.

Puberty

Many decades pass, and the small ones resemble humans or large ones. Standing erect, they are about six to seven feet tall. They are depending if the fin at the back of the head is standing or sagging. Visibly, there is a circle on the chest that is the soul. They have fins on the calf of the legs and behind the elbows. They're helping them maneuver through the seawater swiftly. Their mouths are thick lips and closed most of the time. They are capable of telepathic speaking. Their hands and feet were slight, the fingers and toes webbed. Their ears are crusty with small scales. The breastplate, a shielded area, covers the collarbones and the breast. Leaving the soul spot to reveal the nature of anything with life in the depths. An.

A small rainbow-colored scale is visible. Sheds quickly on those they come into contact with. Coming beneath the oceanic waters to flourish, learning ways to make things happen since they are super intelligent. Knowing the ways of the sea becomes beneficial to them. Time slips by until we count them as Wobbaquas. A name describing their slightly wobbly walking pattern. One which comes and goes at their command. Yet they feel comfortable using it when not in water or on dry land. They can walk just like humans. When in water, the stride differs from humans, especially when they are in the upper world. Gravity plays a part when underwater as they do not exert themselves there—finding some supernatural powers from the soul spot. Decided between the two, not to use the powers unless there is an emergency. Fearful that they could use them up.

Over time and once metamorphosed into seawater surroundings, they were nurtured to life by sea otters. They are bringing forth-year zero for this underwater civilization. They're becoming productive creatures with inner-born characteristics that set them apart in seawater—finding it easy to swim long distances. The maneuver is well in areas of unrest and tidal waves. Many have developed into quite maneuverable sea creatures. Gilled with protrusions that are in places around the body. Those to accept the deep. Leaving their domain of life with the sea otters raised them. They have released the jellyfish into oceanic existence. They know how to navigate. Moving from place to place, they have to watch for ships and submarines. Swimming at astronomical speeds. To the Wobbaquas, water seems like slices of light. Passing swiftly through it, they tend their surroundings. Coming toward them, one might say they are magnificent in stature! There are no gender parts on a Wobbaqua, no male or female.

All Wobbaqua beings of the sea can mate once through puberty. Conceiving through the soul spot from the sensual encounter. It still takes two, and once they breed. "They do not know which one will become impregnated." Therefore, to carry the young one to birth.

The situation is that they have to both agree on the decision to get that way. Coming together as a team will cause this. Again, they know the consequences of their actions. At the same time, many are in the lower quadrants. That of the deep will misuse themselves. Many leave the offspring on the roadside to be devoured by other marine mammals. On the watch out for this behavior, the Mermaids save the day! Evaluating their age and placing them in an appropriate atmosphere for the offspring.

This, in turn, prompts the older ones to go after the parent who had the child—placing them into a disciplinary situation. Many are in prison and never released until the baby dies off. They are waiting until many have some accident or pass away.

Coming into existence daily to revamp. The Wobbaqua, the tallest of the two, comes forward, lying upon the beach that seems to be endless. Warm sand is inviting at sunrise, capturing some rays and feeling like swimming ten miles. In all reality, coming into play may be hormones. Laying still might relieve some of the anxiety that comes. Innocence and other factors get into it.

The emotions. Then, the community daycare centers, for those thrown out by the jellyfish and filled with many little ones. Clatter fills the depths energetically as they are jumping, singing, smiling, and excited to be alive.

"Why! The singing rings loudly through the seawater, reflecting happiness throughout the surrounding area." Millennial said.

Soundproof walls keep the singing room sounding like a distress call to the animals and fish in the ocean water. Not to alarm anyone. They don't want predators coming for the helpless little ones.

We thrive off of keeping all the food fed. Feeding many little ones comes at a price. The wheelbarrow is complete. Supply and demand bring the grubs in. Many babies Wobbaquas take sucks from their mermaid surrogate mommas. Thousands are not old enough to ingest the daily diet of grubs. Among the thousands placed in daycare, they are being put into community care. It seems some of the older children eat kelp from the seabed.

Many large troughs at the local farmers' market have turnip greens. Seaworthy Porta potties are built-in random places. For the community to use. Babies of a certain age are content inside massively large jellyfish; therefore, they are learning.

Placed there to become older and fed a lifetime of knowledge. Not gender worthy, they provided them for the future. Farmers deliver some foodstuff straight to the daycare. Therefore, to cut out the middleman. Workers blend the kelp and grubs.

We consider any worm that lives in a marine environment a marine worm. We find marine worms in several phyla, including the Platyhelminthes, Nematoda, Annelida, Chaetognatha, hemichordates, and Phoronida. For a list of marine animals called "sea worms", Make many bottles from shells creatively for the babies to feed easily.

Some babies are allergic to the mixture. Many get scours and gas from ingesting it. With everything, they bring the baby back until this condition is under control. Water housing builds up the baby's stamina. Therefore, the development of fins and healthy gills becomes a must. Development helps them in navigating through their lives. Many children have to pass a test to be sent home. Living on their own, they make it. The mandatory process ensures the safety and longevity of the fittest. Once placed back into the home setting. They survive on their food. Therefore, they make a life for themselves.

Age becomes a factor since a Wobbaqua is half the age of humans in body composition and survival. Many never return to their jellyfish or mermaids. The Wobbaquas that have become teens inside the massive jellyfish take on a different fin type. The expansion of the upper body's growing fins. This brings them to a puberty-type look. Released from the belly of the jellyfish. They are flying above the oceanic waters, maneuvering over choppy water. Should they come close to land? Only the human eye sees them while in flight, spiraling down several hundred feet. This alone can damage them when they plummet.

Humans misconstrued them as flying fish. One thing about becoming a teen Wobbaqua. They have to learn how to handle their new equipment. Learn to navigate; they stay out of harm's way. The gill is behind the head and runs from the crown of the head. Past the mental lobe and down the back of the neck. Furnishing much-needed oxygen from the seawater. Wherever the oxygen comes into the waterway, a long, slinky fin is behind the leg's calf. One that has a gill in-housed in it. Should the Wobbaqua situation be where they cannot get oxygen from the head?

Lower gills of red will surmise life for them. Gills are branching organs on the side of fish heads that have capillaries. Many tiny blood vessels are called capillaries as the Wobbaqua opens its mouth wide. Water runs over the gills, and blood is in the capillaries. They pick up oxygen that's dissolved in the seawater. "Wobbaquas' gills are organs that allow them to breathe underwater. Most marine creatures exchange oxygenated gasses. Similar to or like oxygen and carbon dioxide. Using gills protected under gill covers on both sides of the pharynx (throat). Gills are tissues that are like short threads, protein structures called filaments."

Millennial said. Breathing gills allow them many attributes that some marine animals don't have. Fish transfer oxygen from the seawater to their blood using a highly efficient mechanism called countercurrent oxygen exchange. Countercurrent Exchange means the flow of water over the gills is opposite to the flow of blood through the capillaries in the lamellae.

This is because the blood flowing in the capillaries always encounters water with higher oxygen. The human body needs to function and exhale carbon dioxide as waste. Wobbaquas open the mouth, water runs over the gills, and blood in the back of the gill sack will exchange oxygen to allow the existence of each one. These great little organs enable the fish to absorb oxygen from the water, using it for energy. Functioning more prominent gills are not that dissimilar to the lungs in humans. Same with other mammals. Deriving oxygen from the seawater.

The fundamental difference is how they can absorb much smaller concentrations of oxygen. All the while allowing the fish to maintain an appropriate Sodium Chloride (salt) level in their bloodstream." Millennial explains. Gills work on the same principle as lungs. Small sacs called alveoli in the lungs have approximately 70% capillaries. These capillaries carry deoxygenated blood from the body.

As oxygen and carbon dioxide pass across the alveoli's membrane, the capillaries return the newly oxygenated blood to the body. To treat, combine, or enrich with oxygen. Similarly, gills have small rows and columns of specialized cells grouped closely and called the epithelium. This supplies directly deoxygenated blood to the fish. Coming from the heart to the epithelium via arteries and even smaller arterioles.

As it forces seawater across the epithelium membranes, dissolved oxygen in the seawater is up by tiny blood vessels and veins. At the same time, they exchange carbon dioxide through the gills. Then there are sea water spiders. Many spiders of the sea can jump across a pyramid. The webs crowd the waterways. They are deep purple, blue, and gray.

Their webs are used as nets once the spider finishes feeding from them. Although invisible to the naked eye, they are completely translucent. Wobbaquas can see them. Turning one side causes the visibility of these. They quartered off in the deep spaces between the Bermuda triangle and Africa toward the North American continent, out of the way of Wobbaquas traveling through the waters at astronomical speeds. The spiders feed on the isopods when they can find them.

The mother spiders carry the young on their backs. Should Wobbaquas fall prey to one, they will consume meat in a few seconds? I call them acid spiders. Millennial has a way of making them do what he sees best. They may benefit from the war against the cartel with the isopod mines. They riddle the seafloor with spider eggs. They hatch, and the babies grow fast upon the mother spider's back. Coming into their area of the sea is spine-tingling. “Makes my skin crawl!” Millennial said. “Every habitat has to have a spider in it. These are the gigantic ones. Ha-ha.” Millennial said.

Chapter Two
Where They Went?

Centuries pass rather quickly to the Millennial. The year is 2077, while Millennial and Orbital Man developed a new world for all Wobbaquas. Deep within the abyss of hidden domes. A civilization of millions developing to live beneath the ocean, unnoticed and untouched. They thrive as loving one another so much that they lay down their lives for the survival of all. Traveling the abyss, they grow abundantly after thousands of years. They are developing a lexicon of knowledge spoken by all. Ruled by the Holy One, they cecum to light, a twinkle, a misty, for they know when the mystical ruler has come to them as their king. They are magnifying their belief, turning their attention toward the father.

The mighty one. Never questioning authority, they thrive because the sea opens its bosom to them. Always establish all their needs. They set civilization up as a democracy. There is a judicial system to be operated on daily. The father, who is invisible among the Wobbaquas, rules the Universe. Not all Wobbaquas are sweet and innocent. Now and then, they will bring a few to justice. The warm waters off the coastline of Old Mexico in the Pacific bring forth the colonies.

Underwater for centuries is the city of Atlantis. It struck Atlantis to sink below the ocean when a gigantic volcano erupted. An underwater world abandoned by any life. Has become home to many of the Wobbaquas. It strengthened them through the millennium. They build a beautiful city beneath the ocean. A beautifully designed aquatic city. One that can hold water, those they us daily. They are grown where any life can exist. They are used for the life of the Wobbaqua society. They develop a variety of plants grown, specifically in oceanic greenhouses.

Lettuce, spinach, kale, and mustard greens will all thrive in a greenhouse in the depths. You can also produce other cool-weather crops there, like carrots, beets, peas, and broccoli. For a long-term addition, consider asparagus. These plants can provide you with a continual harvest for up to two years at a time, all grown in the dome's areas of a majestic greenhouse. The crop they grow all the time.

There are many in the vast seabed. Open fields on the seabed's direct sunlight to the seabed plants. Looking at the different kinds of food sources. Tropical, while others are trees and grass. Wide varieties of turnips are all kinds of foliage strewn on the sea beds. Open to sunlight to harvest plants for the open domes.

Grown beneath the exterior of the Wobbaqua world and the closed domes are miles of gardens. They cannot encompass the Wobbaqua world in water. Some areas are differently structured.

The meat source is the small shellfish of the sea.

These areas stand out as being for the transformed. Ones that walk upright are to be transformed into a humanoid form.

Millennial men will be the workers and managers of the whole massive civilization. Predestination to become a mega civilization. Nothing gets past Millennials.

Orbital man will guard the pods and the keeper of the king's room, where all the telecommunication from the father comes into the domes beneath the abyss.

Babies are born to the ones who find love for another. By joining the life portals, they become impregnated. Many new lives have come about. While baby Wobbaquas habitation dwellers unite in a joint agreement. Love has them joining as one soul portal and becoming impregnated. Making new aquatic life, they share the experience. Today, we look back across nineteen hundred years and ask. "What kind of trail have these left across the centuries?"

When we try to sum up his influence. All the armies that ever marched, all the parliaments that ever sat. All the kings that ever reigned are Picayune in their influence on humanity. Compared with that of this one solitary life. The one of the Wobbaquas. This society functions in secret beneath the abyss. Then, we see the reason for the uncovering of this beautiful society. Millennials and Orbital have a job before them and need the services of a human. Requesting help, they intend to rid their world of a newfound predator.

"Seems the humans from the big city of New York have violated our world!" Millennial said.

"They have harvested and distributed a drug that comes only from the dust from isopod fields. One that grows one they are harvesting in the depths of caverns under the sea. This magic dust has half the humans in the large metroplexes in its grip. Besides bringing many Wobbaquas to slavery to get the harvesting of the isopod dust to the surface. This dilemma calls for the services of the New York City police department." Millennial said.

He came with a long array of credentials on his computer. Brick Thunder is our man! The undersea world has sought him out as the one human to trust with their true identity. He alone will help free the teen Wobbaqua who have become enslaved people, beatings of so many."

Millennia continues. "Here are a few qualities this human brings to the table."

Raised Investigator Brick Thunder to attend school in the Bronx of New York, in the United States of America. After high school, Brick attended Curious Community College. Getting his Criminal justice classes in place.

Following up on his law enforcement degree requirements. Taking his enlistment seriously, he becomes a city police officer. He enrolled to get his internship training at a higher accredited college. To enter the police force, he will be ready to train as an investigator. He continued his education until he mastered his weapon and dialog of street slang, besides receiving a Bachelor's degree in law enforcement. Holding his chrome-long barrel, carved Ivory handles 45 pistols to his chest. Brick Thunder is genuinely a marksman. They trained Brick to carry his gun front and center chest. While most wear the holster to the armpit. He has his 38 Smiths and Wesson center chest with a Colt 45 at his hip holstered precisely strapped to his leg. He's one tough fellow.

Resting his hand on the butt of his pistol, he shows off the tattoo on his forearm. Never underestimate his ability to take down a criminal. His expertise in karate is undetermined. Few asses he hasn't cleaned. Brick is like a hound. Once he is on a scent, he will crawl to get his man. Brick entirely cleared most of his crime scenes in a matter of less than a week. Except for this one, one with some from another world completely. Many describe Brick as a tall man who walks tall with broad shoulders and a muscular physique. Many appear at the downtown precinct to capture Brick photos. Being a little elegant, he will pose now and then, especially when a beautiful reporter shows up to snap a few photos.

"Handsome, really handsome," the female reporter said. She was smiling while snapping a few shots of him, watching while entering the precinct today. In his personal life, he keeps to himself and wonders where his heart is. "It's his job." Women come to be with him, yet his mind and soul are with his job. He is stepping into his office days before daylight. The smell of Benhur perfume from the women who work there is stifling, and he is pouring his coffee to start the day. He will never mention the stifling scent. "Hard to get good help nowadays." He said while stirring in a sugar cube to dissolve. Without error, he will never say a word about it. Brick wouldn't want a suit against him for being a male chauvinist pig. Scratching his butt, he situates his pants before sitting into his red leather, broad-studded, roller foot chair. The desk is so shiny that he has to keep his tinted glasses on his nose.

Running his fingers through his dark, wavy hair. Slick with Butch wax hair gel that smells like ear wax. Fine and handsome, muscular, tall, and just right in appearance. An intelligent man at that and a little witty.

A serious note comes when he is doing his job, however. Sipping his sweet coffee, he looks at the rough look of his desk.

Straightening and situating papers of the last shipment of Isopod dirt shipped into the city. They brought smugglers undercover. Concern for the safety of everyone involved crosses his mind.

"This operation is one of the biggest I have ever seen!"

"I will not punch the clock on this job, Brick swears!"

Watching as the daily officer load comes into his office for their daily dose of Bull squat, he talks. "This needs to be cleared up as soon as possible!" Brick said. "Pardon the loud swearing," Buck said as he turned to look at them.

"If anyone can bust this case, it is me!"

"All you men hear this?"

Standing at his desk and stomping, he hears a rumble as the other officers step back a few steps. Letting this magic man into his place among them.

"I have a stack of evidence that each one of you could take and make at least twenty arrests off of. You know the county needs this to have revenues to care for all, driving up Court-appointed attorney's fees." While recognizing the judicial system's needs.

"The streets are the same, and we must pay officers' salaries." Thunder said. "I enjoy listening to my officers' opinions in most situations. Our early morning Question and Answer sessions revitalize us all. It keeps the air clear and brings about new suggestions. This secret project has me dumbfounded! I swear!" Thunder said.

"Hard to imagine the drama that will come. That coming from us trying to bust this case seeded in the depths of the sea! Small refurbished submarines will be our best friend. The leader will represent the other civilization this morning. Well, you all will be surprised. We have to honor their wishes."

"They are the dominant civilization of the sea, capable of annihilating us all if they desire. With their ability to walk among us undetected, they possess the power to maintain peace in our human world. They choose to reside in their underwater civilization known as the Wobbaqua world, and we must comprehend its significance," Thunder said.

Chapter Three

Crime Rates Rise to reach New York

New York City, adorned with tall buildings and alleyways, greeted visitors with a lack of hospitality. The city dwellers remained solemn and closed off, having experienced various forms of abuse from bystanders. They lived quiet lives, unique to the breed of New Yorkers. Some harbored intense hatred, akin to taxi drivers solely focused on making money.

Transgressions and sin-filled the streets of New York City. Isopod dust permeated the air, causing chaos. Addicts emerged from the shadows at sundown, searching for suppliers who infiltrated the city daily.

People walked like zombies, fearing the consequences of witnessing a crime. One wrong move could become a statistic, discarded behind a building.

Unawareness of one's surroundings could be a blessing. Many chose to mind their business and flee crimes to protect themselves.

New York City was filled with transgressions and sin. The streets are filled with a steady flow of isopod dust. This has caused havoc on the roads. Addicts come out from the shadows and come sundown. Many look for the harvesters who slip into the city to reinfest it daily.

"Prostitution and theft have reached unprecedented levels due to addiction to isopod dust. Many individuals are under its control, contributing to the spread of diseases and turmoil," Brick voiced his concerns. The drug cartels had grown, exploiting society and devastating families like strip clubs. The presence of one would inevitably lead to a dozen more unnoticed until crime escalated, Thunder explained.

Unrecognizable individuals adorned with numerous tattoos, some using ink to cover scars inflicted through street fights. "Gangs and street fighters often need to be subdued forcefully, with sharp objects piercing their skin to keep them on the ground," Thunder mentioned.

"Do we shock them again if they try to escape?" Brick asked, contemplating ways to maintain control over these individuals.

"Many sports vividly colored hair and matching attire, while others conceal themselves under shroud-like coverings due to a virus introduced by foreigners from underdeveloped societies," Thunder noted. "Most people either cover their faces or wear masks to protect themselves, but some willingly spread the virus without remorse," Markel added.

"Markel, I truly appreciate your dedication as my right-hand man in tackling these issues," Inspector Thunder expressed gratitude. "Our goal is to combat crime, meticulously weaving through its organized and deceitful nature. The skyscrapers, towering like roots reaching the clouds, witness our efforts."

"We should be thankful for the vaccines and the society that has successfully fended off most epidemics," Thunder acknowledged.

"It is unacceptable that children must remain confined to their homes to survive. Our society has reached a point where many possess the disposition of mongrels," Brick observed, recognizing the different characteristics defining people's lives.

"That makes my job easier!" Thunder exclaimed, acknowledging the distinctive qualities of individuals.

"Outlying areas are being patrolled since refined women tend to visit malls, increasing crime. Officers armed with guns and lasers walk through the malls, maintaining peace within the community," Thunder explained. "Thieves and shoplifters lurk near the registers, ready to snatch children or an elderly woman's purse. These low-lives take advantage of government assistance that they don't deserve," Thunder expressed his frustration.

"People who only cause havoc in the community while others shop and waste resources," Grady commented. "The constant flow of people creates disturbances in places like malls and shopping centers. Even neighborhoods face food shortages due to individuals stealing and hijacking grocery trucks," Markel shared.

The food pantries meant for people in need become an opportunity for exploitation by some. The narcotic isopod dust threatens to destroy society and drive more people to the streets.

"When such behaviors come to light, the city must take action to prevent organized riots and the destruction of beautiful cities. It serves as an example to the riotous society we face, often controlled by the government," Thunder emphasized.

"We have spotters who risk their lives to protect others, willing to sacrifice themselves to expose the truth. They are a minority in society. One spotter was shot for uncovering illegal activities at the Texas border. This is what our society has come to," Thunder lamented.

"The magnitude of crimes forces Brick to assign ninety officers to patrol the marked barricaded streets of New York City," Thunder admitted. "Office buildings hire security guards to combat repeated assaults, especially against women, men, and children returning home. Multi-level parking garages remain hotspots for crime, instilling fear," Thunder continued.

"To deter criminals and maintain peace within the community, various types of weaponry, painted midnight blue, are utilized. Hover vehicles are employed to curb crime in the city, including the use of shotguns with barrels of the same distinct color. Officers strategically navigate the base of skyscrapers, catching offenders who try to enter apartments from outside windows, molesting people and stealing their hard-earned money," Grady reported. Thunder acknowledged the undercover officers, including Grady, Homer, and Harold, who assisted him.

Abusing them, never to tell how they got inside. Besides, they never passed a security guard. "It seems the city Government has an enormous garage at the waterfront in the Hudson Bay area. Where to house the many types of armored cars and military-type armory?" Homer said. Should they need it, they are ready to use since crime in the inner city has mushroomed." Homer continued.

Markel turned the corner to the judicial complex. The bright blue Hoovers' hound vehicle hums right at the door. Looking up, Thunder stands feeling dignified, watching as they maneuver to the height of the building's first steps. Then, rounding things off. Thunder steps out to walk closer to the Hudson Bay area.

"Flying around low and quiet in a custom-made hoover hound dog. One designed to do what thunder wants to do! Investigate and sneak around." Markel said.

"With so many skyscrapers at the edge of the bay area, they have to be careful. Knowing people are being guarded. Many are guarded by heavily dressed military-style gear. Resembling that on his officers in the hummer lowrider." Whew! Chester said.

"Stepping in closer, he watches as many slip into the invisibility of the edge of the buildings. Watching while the only man alive who can conquer the situation is right before the hoodlums. Suddenly, shooting comes from a distance directed towards Thunder. Dropping to his belly, he crawls across to one pylon that is at the edge of the bay. Sliding beneath the dock for cover." Chester told me.

He listens as his fleet of men tracks down the shooter. Once they have him, the hummer brings Thunder up from the edge of the pylons beside the seawall. Bringing him into the hummer they park to give him cover should there be another shooter!

Loading then re-holstering his weapon into the scalbert on his chest. Thunder places bullets in the chamber. Slowly slide it across the smooth brown leather holster to snap it into place. With a pull from the scalbert, the weapon's safety is hot, loaded, and ready to shoot.

“Should he hit anything with his Colt 45-long barrel pistol, he will blow a hole the size of a kitchen coffee saucer?

Markel started ribbing the engine because they were ready.” Markel said.

Readied for what the day brings, Markel stands tall. Looking through the heavy, dark-tinted, bulletproof windows of the hummer as they arrive safely.

He returned to the judicial complex to finish his day at work. Walking tall, Thunder enters the building to recap what just took place! Making out a police report has to be precise and legible. All written material that goes to be filed in any legal form must be without any mistakes.

Thunder is determined that his officers make all necessary changes. “Those to accommodate the rightful filing of all documents from his office as absolutely correct!”

Resting in his job, Inspector Thunder awaits Millennial coming to him. Therefore helping uncover these culprits that riddle the world with drugs and destruction of lives.

"Ensure the Millennial man is directed to my office," Inspector Thunder instructed. "Just like my tracks leave a mark in the sand, telling a story, the track of a snake reveals where it was and where it is going," Thunder mused. The Wobbaquas, through their arsenal, displayed their readiness to defend their right to live in peace. They must unite to protect their freedom.

The precinct personnel sensed Thunder's nervousness, evident in his increased talking.

Chapter Four
Aquatic Weapons

Millennial is prepared to advance in the war against the villains, ready to take action. Like the opening of a vault, the side of a distant mountain reveals an arsenal. The Millennial man flips a switch, granting sight to a magical world of weapons.

As the water departs from the opening, a pale aqua-blue mist envelops the vast area—the trees' part, unveiling a gap in the soil. Stepping into the blissful portal, they discover an abundance of weaponry emerging from the rest of the mountain. Curiosity arises about the number of beautiful golden archery pieces lined up on a ledge adorned with golden feather fins at the tip of each arrow.

These exquisite arrows are embellished with fancy laced, floppy seaweed and flowing barnacles. Row after row, arrow pouches are neatly arranged on the side. They are securely strapped with the finest leather sourced from seals. Describing the organization as systematic would be an understatement. The ammunition within is of magical ampleage, making it highly valuable. The dome-shaped rock formation of the hidden cave's exterior is covered in blue moss.

This moss acts as a barrier, preventing barnacles and other substances from adhering to the stones. Consequently, the cave remains sealed as the moss inhibits their attachment. There is something in the blue rock moss that prevents sticking.

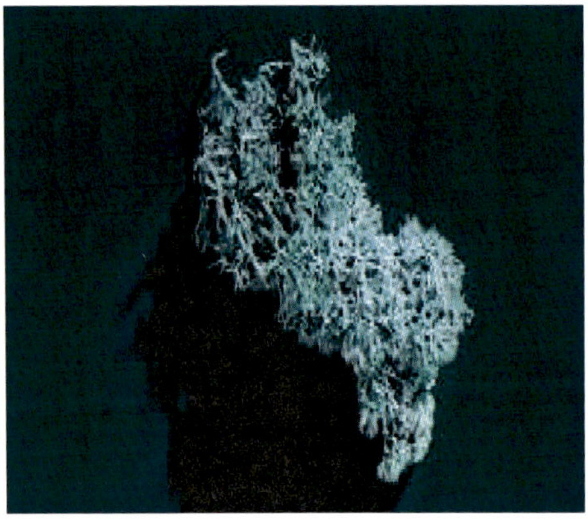

What is Blue Sea Moss?

Sea moss, scientifically known as Chondrus crispus, is **algae or seaweed**. It grows in waters along the rocky Atlantic coasts, primarily between North America and Europe.[1] It's an edible sea plant similar to other seaweeds, algae, and other familiar leafy sea vegetables like kelp or dulse.

This also keeps the aquatic life away, as it will not feel or hold barnacles or shellfish. This keeps sharks. Like man-eating fish away from the area that houses the weaponry. Leaving a way

[1] (Panoff, 2021)

for entrance. Coming into the massive encrypted cave. Occupied by those who need ammunition. Those who live beneath the depths. Those are called Wobbaquas.

Weaponry

Mechanical means generate scalding hot water, which can cause explosive reactions when in contact. These Kubas can engulf an entire area of villains, leaving behind only an empty underwater space.

These grenades, crafted from chemicals extracted from whale blubber and containing nitro, create chaos upon pulling the pin. They have a reputation for bringing down towering oceanic structures.

Bullets of crushed shells bound by resin firmly secure their target. They contain feathered lead inside, ready to explode upon contact with anything other than water.

Numerous vehicles can traverse underwater and airborne realms at the speed of light. Adorned in various colors, they possess a magical ability to blend seamlessly with their surroundings.

Many ideas stem from the cylinders deep within the domes, ensuring safety. These ideas include spears twice the length of a man, intended for throwing or shooting from loaded cannons.

Once thrown, the mechanism can transform the spear into a deadly projectile, as seen with this particular weapon.

A cannon-like Uzi, mounted on the razor mobile, can traverse water with force. There is also arm gear capable of causing explosions from a distance.

"Telepathic signals cause the water to open like gates, and then there are moon gates. These gates form when aliens from other galaxies enter the realm of oceanic waters. Millennia have designed them with the mystical knowledge passed down by their fathers. They are formed from deep reflections of slithered blue moonbeams within the obis, creating openings into nothingness. Each gate exists within the diameter of the Wobbaqua civilization. Any Wobbaqua can seek protection by entering one."

"These gates can be closed and locked in the same manner. A palm wand button enables Wobbaquas to become invisible on command. Radar systems track the activities of all Wobbaquas during times of war. The armory has been revolutionized to transport individuals between illuminated locations. Module-type spheres called water zippers have been designed to safeguard anything needing protection. They are particularly valuable for preserving precious lives, especially during impending explosions. Watercraft of the highest quality fills the arsenal of fighters."

"The invisible sea-hound seacraft was developed, originating from the casing left behind by the aliens at the top of the pyramid. No one saw it except for Millennials, who stored it for later use. When he grew up, he recalled that it had been left at the edge of the Sea of Galilee. 'Millennial never wastes anything,' Orbital remarked. Millennials share details about a few of the weaponry they possess."

"These hovercraft water wagons prove invaluable for sea creatures that lack the magical ability to traverse water at high speeds. Bucklebacks and other species benefit from them as well. In the event of a war, these hovercrafts are crucial. They can swiftly transport machinery through the water at extraordinary speeds, capable of traveling on a beam of light that penetrates and extends across the water. Atomic-powered air blasters are utilized as large-scale seabed bombs. They are meticulously designed to avoid overturning domes or causing harm to surrounding structures, solely intended for clearing debris such as aquatic life or anything smaller than large turtles—all under the protection of others."

"The purpose is for Wobbaquas to sacrifice themselves for the survival of younger generations. This is the law that maintains the balance of the aquatic world." Millennial continues.

"The security of the aquatic realm is entrusted to a special breed of Wobbaquas born to protect. Unseen by most, they are both humble and distinguished, committed to serving and safeguarding." Millennial concludes, "Daily security measures benefit sea-dwelling not only creatures but also any intruders who enter the area, as they fall under the protection of the Shots—elder members of the Wobbaqua society."

Searching for remnants of sunken sailing ships containing usable materials can be stressful. It's hard to resist the allure of a good history lesson. A shipwreck is believed to be Blackbeard's ship, as indicated by the writing across its bow. It is located nearby, and we can utilize some of the remaining artillery to aid in the upcoming battle. "Remind me to inform Fishman that we should visit Fishman Island!" he exclaimed.

There are many styles of businesses in their life, lined up in a row for grandeur. Before the cusp of the moon, there will be a magnificent parade. We will see many who have employed our new weaponry. The vehicles have been hired and developed for Millennials. This type of battle will involve the isopod. As the days slip past, the moon changes. They were lined up at the back of the city while all the militia sat dormant. Some come from schools, and others from local driving aquatic equipment. There are floats and many other shows depicting the civilization of the Wobbaquas. The water churns as each high-powered vehicle eases closer to the lineup.

The Fish man jumps up and down in excitement, looking at what he has developed from nothing. These are the gifts the sea has provided for all. Children float beside the city's roadways, not walking but in mid-stream. They take in the grandeur of the magnificent parade. All the floats and ammunition vehicles fill locker garages. This show of excellence is meant to showcase the Aquatic world's efforts against the intruders in the abyss.

Morning arrives as the floats move through the streets lined with thousands of Wobbaquas. Everyone watches in awe at the beautiful mermaid displays. The children are on some floats, surrounded by lights and excitement. Some floats are made with the magic of the sea, stretched on long trailers. One of them displays a giant clamshell and a pearl the size of a washtub, released from the temple's vault. It is the largest one in captivity in the Wobbaqua world. The floating floor is covered with sea glass and pink shrimp shells. Inside the pink shells, many children's Wobbaquas sit. Parents place each child-like little pearl in the big clam shells. As the floats ease through the chosen route, Millennial and his counterpart Orbital stand at a distance, witnessing the grandeur. "Once this ends, we will house these weapon vehicles inside the domes until the battle begins. There, we will take back our world of peace," Millennial continues. Then we can have a war museum.

Speaking softly, Orbital says, "I agree, brother. We know what we are doing and will reclaim what is ours. Meanwhile, the upper world can stay away from the life we know." Orbital adds, "The battle will begin and end in our favor."

We plan to carry through and show the world what and who governs this seawater world. Peace and harmony are our top priorities! If fighting keeps our world a secret for another thousand years, then war is!" Orbital declares.

The weaponry consists of knives that slice through water like watermelons, extracting the juice effortlessly. Sling Blades carry water waves to new destinations. Perfectly formed gunpowder-filled balls are used as cannonballs, exploding upon reaching the ocean floor within a fraction of a second. The vehicles resemble the depths and are made of bronzed steel, shimmering with a golden aqua color. Their laced paint never deteriorates as they blast through war zones without harming anyone behind them. The wheels are white onyx rock, and the overhead roll bars are from whale jawbones. Many extras are derived from the magic of the Wobbaqua capsules, including definitive buttons within the fins of the Wobbaquas, determining the fate of the war-ridden plains beneath the ocean.

There are also vehicles strewn with cylinders made of crab shells and empty housings from days gone by, scattered like breadcrumbs to pigeons with memories of times past.

Millennial Man, named today, gazes at the entrance to the Capitol dome of Wobbaqua City. He notices a seeping crack in the structure that needs immediate attention, especially before the tropical depression emerges off the coast of Africa. The massive force could warp the dome and cause further damage if it becomes a hurricane. "Though structurally sound, the threat remains," he continues. "Yes, we will repair all of this," Millennial says, delivering a lecture to the dome inhabitants at Wobbaqua College. He explains his latest invention, a threaded seatbelt.

"We will have seatbelts threaded for all Wobbaquas who wish to wear them! Many will be for the mermaids to protect the innocent and safeguard the Wobbaqua mermaid world. These seatbelts will be specially designed for the mother mermaids' surrogates," Millennial explains. He returns to his laboratory, where he designs a belt that serves as a safety seatbelt, sticking to the shoulder of a mermaid and allowing her to reach her sword instantly. The belt also contains a compartment for communication housed within a lining of self-healing chemicals.

Additionally, it features a magical wound healer, a sharp ice pick-like object with multiple uses. The backpack carrying the belt is lightweight and transparent, with only the wearer knowing its uses. Millennial concludes his speech, stating that the training for using these seatbelts will be offered exclusively to mermaids, with no others allowed in the college classes for this specific course.

The remainder of the speech is left to the Millennial's brother, Orbital, who steps onto the podium to finalize the war plans. "As the warrior of the sea, let me elaborate on this topic. My role here is to refresh everyone in the underwater environment," Orbital announces, marking the clouds with deep and insightful words. At the same time, his magnificent galactic outfit shines like a polished silver spoon in the sky above the oceanic waters.

The helmet of sea existence is the foundation upon which the warrior stands. When placed on one's head, it magically penetrates the minds of all who wear it. However, it is kept in a vault to prevent damage to the ecosystem of the depths in case it falls into the hands of the strong.

I carefully strapped the inscribed **sword of the sea warrior** into a leather sharkskin pouch hanging from his waist. This sword has been used countless times to attack the enemies of the sea, and the warrior wears it with pride. The sword's beautiful design is evident, as it was hammered from iron ore found in the caves beneath the Mariana plates, which hold the world together. Each underwater sword is adorned with precious stones, braided with brass wire. The handle is a masterpiece, with diamonds, rubies, and emeralds enhancing its beauty. The sword's blade is crafted from a shark's jawbone and transformed into a magical weapon through the skillful work of a millennial man.

The belt of truth symbolizes the warrior's adherence to the laws of the seawater world. It is worn around his waist, displaying his superiority to all who traverse the underwater realm alongside his brother.

The breastplate of righteousness protects from the evils lurking in the seawater. It shields the wearer's soul spot, making the surrounding areas appear safe when worn upon the chest.

The shield of faith extinguishes the darts of evil that hide in the depths. These weapons are forged using hot vats in the deep sea. It is said that liquid mercury plays a role in their production, and when mixed with nitro, they have the power to move mountains. These shields explode with an incredibly powerful force field.

Recent findings indicate that mercury is being extracted from sailfish to produce isopod dust, which is used in creating weaponry. Scientists in the millennial world of the Wobbaquas have discovered this process. Still, it is causing harm to the sea's ecosystem. As a result, swordfish populations are declining, creating a void in the food chain for humans and the aquatic world of the Wobbaquas. Unfortunately, this war has driven the development of impressive weaponry by aquifer manufacturers.

The handles of these pistols and swords are made of twisted wire containing mercury. When a pistol is fired, the weight of the mercury propels it forward, activating the nitro within the shells. This leads to a massive explosion upon impact. These handguns can be carried on the elbow, providing a wide range of protection for the warriors. Being underwater, the warriors appreciate the lightness of these weapons, which are holstered on their arms and can be electronically triggered with a simple thought from the Wobbaqua wearing them. Warehouses are stocked with various types of weaponry in anticipation of the war.

As the sea-prodding finned feet move, they leave a trail of goodness behind with each step.

Secret Places

The orbital man diligently guards the massive domed structure that houses the father of all spirits and oversees the management of everything beneath the oceanic waters. The Wobbaqua civilization has adopted sea glass and diamonds, harvested by their authoritative figures, as their currency. Hidden beneath the surface lies the silent abyss, where diamond and sea glass mines reside. Within the city, gates and pyramids serve as repositories for the true wealth of the civilization. The entrances to the mines are concealed behind the pyramids, where diamonds are shaped and polished, sea glass is molded, and coins are created for use in their monetary system.

The color of the seagrass predicts the value of a coin, and they imprinted the dime with a mermaid holding a baby on it. At the same time, a two-dollar bill has nothing but a handprint on it.

- Green is for a silver dollar in human change.
- Red is for a fifty-cent piece,
- Precise is for a dollar, while
- Marble Color is for the quarter
- The Nickel has a water buffalo on it.
- Pennies are just sand dollar-shaped.

Information scarcity is crucial to protect the secret society, as revealing its existence could lead humanity to the wrong place. Therefore, individuals are carefully chosen from birth and sworn to dedicate their lives to safeguarding and preserving the value of the hidden mines. They commit themselves to prevent any harm that may befall the Wobbaquas. While these individuals may have families and lead everyday lives, they are bound by strict secrecy. They must never disclose the whereabouts of the treasures within the aquatic world. They must always be vigilant of those who approach. Their role is to ensure the foolproof functioning of the underwater civilization. These underwater warriors lead dual lives, responsible for keeping the underwater world functioning smoothly. They access chambers Within the pyramids with sliding glass portals leading to the mine entrances. When pressurized, the mines open, revealing vast rooms with green and translucent walls teeming with thriving sea life. From the outside, these walls appear as massive underwater rocks.

Upon arriving at the entrance to the hidden mines, there are two diamond crystal bookends. Between these bookends lies a map that guides the journey to another aquatic world. However, only Millennial men are allowed to move this sacred artifact. Suppose the seal on the binder is broken. In that case, it will enable space travelers to return there and explore the various nationalities of Wobbaquas, experiencing the differences in their cultures.

The holy grail, representing the map and its significance, is kept under the strictest security measures. It can only be activated by reading the palm of the designated Wobbaqua, who holds the honor of opening the minds of others. Two exquisitely shaped diamonds of the highest quality found in the sea are positioned on the outer ends of the bookends. These diamonds illuminate when touched, indicating whether the doors to the mines have been opened for the day. They remain invisible to all except the one who has the authority to unlock the gate to the mines.

The bookends serve multiple purposes. They can be turned on pivots to release the life cycle of the Wobbaqua race, representing the sacred knowledge and wisdom passed down through generations. Additionally, they are used to open the doors of the mint area. However, these bookends have been left untouched for eternity, as fewer Millennials or Orbital individuals desire to disrupt their hiding place, knowing that doing so would turn their world upside down. It is a momentous event that is never intended to occur.

The Mint

When the diamond crystal bookends are slid together, they unlock the door to the mines. Inside, the mines serve as the Fort Knox of the Wobbaqua world.

It is in this area where the machines responsible for producing sea glass coins and diamonds for the money exchange are located. The purpose of this entire setup is to facilitate the creation of these valuable resources.

At a large table crafted from pure emerald, several elderly Wobbaquas can be found. They are adorned in white linen robes and wear hooded cloaks embellished with fine stones along the sleeves and hem. Despite their advanced age, they possess an inevitable frailty. The scarcity of honesty necessitates keeping them engaged in their role to maintain their integrity. Dedication to their craft also plays a part in upholding their commitment.

Their task is to squeeze the sea glass and transform it into what can be considered man-made diamonds. Each diamond is created for specific purposes, and if not designated for such, they are fired and cut to become genuine diamonds, which hold even greater value in money exchanges. Only certain Wobbaquas can perform this procedure, as they approach it from a place of necessity rather than greed. The experience and expertise of these elder Wobbaquas result in the production of the most sought-after coins of the highest quality.

However, it is essential to note that should one's heart grow cold and their desire to mold diamonds become driven by greed, the father figure, who deeply understands the individual's soul, can discern their true nature.

Those driven by greed are swiftly removed from the group in this aquatic world. The "Wearever" men, dedicated workers responsible for keeping the mines operational, enter the scene and empty a basket of uncut diamonds onto the table. The older Wobbaquas smile, knowing that they have a task at hand. A "Wearever" man is described as a seven-foot-tall Wobbaqua with a massive muscular build and thick scales acquired from wildlife. Many of these individuals have faced hardships and have been prematurely separated from the knowledge bank of the jellyfish, leaving them lacking in certain areas of knowledge. However, there is a place in the depths for everyone in this society.

The Wearevers spend their entire lives working to sustain the mines. It is mentioned that lacking formal education can put individuals in difficult circumstances throughout life. While some educated individuals may withhold valuable information from those less informed, others continue learning and are willing to help others achieve their dreams for the sake of their families. However, the narrative emphasizes that it is rare for a Wearever to rise in the aquatic society's hierarchy.

Comparisons are drawn between the Wearevers and trash collectors or individuals who handle deceased bodies in the upper world. The idea is that everyone has a place in this society, regardless of their educational background. Education is not a prerequisite for these positions, as the ocean takes care of itself in most cases. "Wearevers" describes those expelled prematurely from the jellyfish and have not completed their knowledge cycle.

The mine dwellers, who live near the mines and often have their own homes, form a significant part of this society. Different types of Wobbaquas are destined for their unique lifestyles; some are born with inherent abilities suited for the depths due to their time spent inside the jellyfish, while others possess talents for different tasks. However, all function together as an aquatic society.

The City

The Allegader colonies serve as guardians of the Wobbaqua civilization. These colonies are large, mysterious gadgets that appear in a situation of danger. The Wobbaquas have developed into a new group of sea-bearing creatures, and their city is built with scattered sea glass domes. These domes are designed to withstand the elements of nature and even encounters with migrating whales. The domes provide housing for the Wobbaquas, with each dome covering a significant area and being made of thick sea glass that can repel shark attacks.

Within the city are guards dressed in heavy artillery attire, specifically trained to ensure safety. They carry walkie-talkie radios and act as protectors of the domes. If the crowns are ever penetrated, they emit a radiating color to indicate the breach. The inner city of the Wobbaqua world is called "Philiffi," where the upper-class Wobbaquas reside. Protecting the domes and the entire town is paramount to everyone living beneath the seawater.

The guards, known as Millennial men, possess special tools and weapons. They carry Tommy Hawk hatchets with sharkskin scalberts on their hips. These hatchets have twenty-four hollowed-out gunpowder-filled shark teeth aligned on their belts. By striking the tooth with the hammer side of the hatchet, an explosion can be triggered, deterring any threats to the Wobbaquas.

There are dangers in the deep divide where isopod fields are found, and some Wobbaquas have become slaves to illegal chemical removal. Millennial men come to the rescue, working to prevent harm to their fellow Wobbaquas and ensuring their freedom. They intervene when outsiders threaten the aquatic city and collaborate with leaders from both worlds to address and clean up any issues.

Millennial man, a significant figure in this society, practices meditation to find himself in the eternal now, helping him cope with his challenges. He recognizes the involvement of organized crime and law enforcement in the inner city. He aims to protect the Waterworld from human intrusion. The inner city is located near fault lines and the Mariana Trench's crevices, making it a dangerous area for submarines. The entrance to the city of "Philiffi" is marked by two golden statues of one-hundred-foot Wobbaqua figures, each holding a bone spear. The golden statues shine magnificently, signifying the grand entrance to the city.

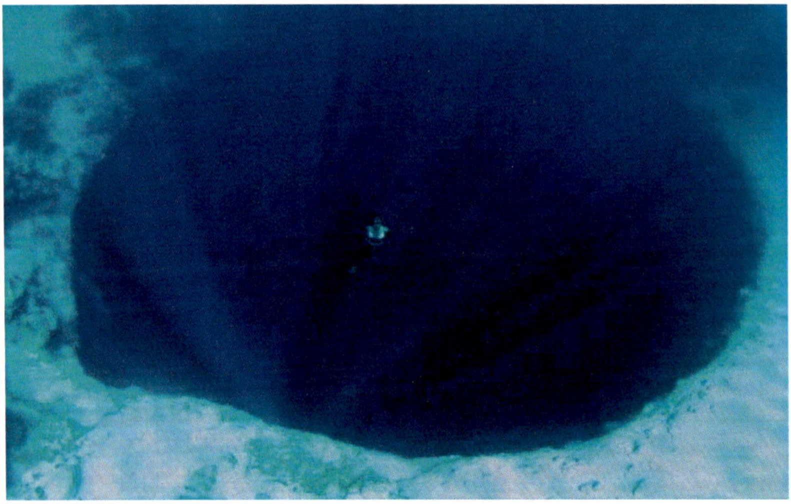

The recent discovery of intact fruit baskets at Thonis-Heracleion, an ancient Egyptian port city located in the bay of Abu Qir, has captivated the attention of researchers and the public. The town, dating back to the 12th century BC and serving as Egypt's primary port until the rise of Alexandria, has remained underwater and untouched for approximately 2,400 years.

The fruit baskets, believed to date back to the 4th century BC, were found during research at Thonis-Heracleion. The precise reason for their preservation is still unknown. Still, it is speculated that they may have been buried within an underground room or intentionally placed there soon after being offered.

There is an intriguing suggestion that the Millennial Wobbaquas, the underwater society, may have played a role in preserving and perhaps even purposefully placing these artifacts for humanity to discover. The find has generated significant interest and excitement, keeping researchers and enthusiasts busy exploring and studying these ancient relics.

The presence of such ancient artifacts highlights the rich history and cultural significance of Thonis-Heracleion and provides valuable insights into the past. The discovery serves as a reminder of the hidden treasures beneath the waters, waiting to be unveiled and shared with humanity.

The discovery of petrified wicker baskets filled with various fruits, including doum nuts and ancient Egyptian grape seeds, adds to the richness of the artifacts found in the submerged ruins of Thonis-Heracleion. These artifacts provide insights into the ancient culture and sacred practices associated with the African palm tree and its fruits.

"Thonis-Heracleion: Wiped Out by Earthquakes and Tidal Waves"

Thonis-Heracleion, once Egypt's largest port on the Mediterranean, experienced a series of natural disasters that eventually led to its submergence. Starting in the 2nd century BC and intensifying in the 8th century AD, earthquakes and tidal waves caused a significant portion of the Nile delta, encompassing a 42-square-mile (110-square-kilometer) area, to collapse under the sea. Thonis-Heracleion, combined with Egyptian and Greek influences, including sanctuaries built by Greek settlers near the temple of Amun, disappeared beneath the waves.

For many years, the existence of Thonis-Heracleion remained forgotten until its rediscovery two decades ago. The ongoing archaeological exploration of this submerged city has yielded remarkable findings, making it one of the most captivating underwater archaeological sites in recent history.

As Millennial and his team continue their work, they know the need to extract valuable resources from the sea to combat the challenges posed by the "demons of the sea." One of these resources involves a powder derived from the ocean's caves, which is being utilized in the city among humans. The Wobbaquas have discovered and left many of these caves untouched, which also contained hidden chambers that housed human remains.

The collaboration between Millennial and his team, along with the Wobbaquas, aims to protect the underwater world, uncover ancient artifacts, and address the misuse of resources by specific individuals. Their efforts contribute to a better understanding of history, culture, and the delicate balance between humanity and the underwater realm.

This is an underwater waterfall that goes into a deep chasm. The waterfall's strong current can pull swimmers into its depths before they realize what is happening. How strong the ocean can be and how quickly it can overpower someone is unbelievable.

With his exceptional investigative skills, Investigator Brick Thunder emerges as the protagonist in the battle against the underwater drug cartel and the harvesting of the destructive isopod dust drug from the ocean floor. Along his journey, he discovers love and support from a Millennial man who understands the responsibilities of protecting their underwater civilization and keeping humans away from their colonies of Wobbaquas.

The Wobbaquas, under Millennial man's guidance, play a crucial role in safeguarding their kind and the valuable resources found in the oceanic depths. They employ advanced weaponry from shark jaws, and barnacle deposits to protect themselves from harm. Their domed city is shielded by radar systems powered by moonbeams, ensuring their safety from intruders.

The Wobbaquas have also repurposed parts from shipwrecks to defend the innocent and have designed great ships crafted from wood and shells for safe travel through treacherous waters. They rely on the assistance of water cats, which guard their territories and exhibit lightning-fast movements underwater.

While chaos ensues outside the city gates, with entertaining encounters involving water cats, giant caterpillars, and worms, the Wobbaqua civilization remains secure within its hidden community. The city of Patiffi believed to be the oldest underwater city, lies off the southern coast of New York and has served as an archeological treasure trove since its discovery in 1967.

The domed cities, located about 500 miles in tropical waters, are named accordingly based on their water temperatures. The largest among them sits close to the Mariana Trench. At the same time, another significant dome is found near the coast of Mexico, close to the location once known as Atlantis. The shifting tectonic plates off the coastline of California caused the sinking of Atlantis 5,000 years ago, resulting in the demise of an entire civilization.

Orbital man, the guardian of the gate to reality and the father dome housed beneath the sea in the great pyramid shares his prophecies with Millennial man, emphasizing his role as a warrior in the battle for the freedom of the Wobbaqua world. A magical throttle handle beside the entrance to their civilization and domes holds a golden key that will aid Millennial men in understanding the upcoming challenges.

Together, Investigator Brick Thunder, Millennial Man, and the Wobbaquas strive to overcome the threats posed by the drug cartel and protect their underwater civilization. As they face unexpected dangers, they remain resolute in their fight for freedom and to preserve their oceanic home.

Millennial man provides insight into the isopod beds and their significance within the Wobbaqua civilization. Isopods, also known as "curly ques" in the upper worlds, are tiny creatures that inhabit the depths beneath the Wobbaqua city domes. These isopods serve as the source of the valuable chemicals derived from them.

The isopod seedbeds are located near the channels below the hot water vents, where these lifelike creatures thrive in the depths. Unfortunately, some individuals have turned to the illegal drug trade, harvesting the chemicals derived from isopods for personal profit.

Beneath the seawater currents, the Wobbaqua civilization treasures the wealth and resources found within these isopod beds. The significance of the isopods and their chemical derivatives is highly valued among the Wobbaquas, and their harvesting is tightly regulated to ensure the preservation of their underwater world.

As the Millennial man explains, the Orbital man, adorned in majestic attire featuring rustic diamonds, jewels, and a crown of solid gold, represents true royalty. His appearance is accentuated by studded stones embedded in his head fin, displaying his royal status. The presence of the crown is reserved for special occasions when the Millennial man and his counterpart are present, emphasizing their mutual appreciation for royalty and the importance of their roles within the Wobbaqua civilization. Together, they recognize the significance of the isopod beds and the need to protect their resources from those who seek to exploit them for personal gain. Their focus remains on preserving the integrity of their underwater kingdom and safeguarding the valuable treasures beneath the sea.

The situation described involves "organized crime" and drug cartels operating within the Wobbaqua civilization. The drug cartel's arrival in New York City raises concerns among news broadcasters and society, as their presence advertises the availability of isopod dust, which fuels crime rates. Unmarked graves along backroads serve as a grim reminder of those who fell victim to the dangerous drug trade.

Brick Thunder, the chief investigator of the New York City police force, becomes involved in the case as those associated with the upper world come into contact with the Wobbaqua mafia and the isopod beds. The Wobbaquas, who possess unique capabilities to withstand the underwater vents' heat and deep-sea pressure, are enslaved by the mafia to work in the isopod fields.

To combat the situation, Millennial men and their Aquatic army seek to free their people from slavery and protect their underwater world. Legionnaires, a well-trained underwater military force with magical weaponry and knowledge from galaxy travelers, join the battle to defend their realm and eradicate the drug trade.

Inspector Brick Thunder focuses on stopping the production and distribution of drugs within New York City, aiming to eradicate the havoc caused by addiction and crime. He understands that those desperate for the isopod drug turn to a life of crime to obtain it, emphasizing its destructive impact on humanity.

As the investigation progresses, Inspector Thunder recognizes potential corruption at the corporate level in the drug distribution network. He aims to follow the leads and bust the case open, bringing all those involved to justice.

Training dolphins to detect isopod dust in seawater becomes a potential strategy to aid in the investigation, utilizing confiscated vehicles and seeking assistance from the Wobbaquas to access deeper parts of the ocean.

The ultimate goal is to dismantle the organized crime network, protect the Wobbaqua civilization, and rid the city of the devastating drug trade that has infiltrated society. Inspector Brick Thunder remains determined to bring all those involved to justice and restore order to the community.

Chapter Five

Breeding

Breeding and pod dropping are gender-neutral activities, with no specific genitalia involved. Either gender can drop pods to initiate the birth of new life. These unique beings reside beneath the ocean's waters, where they acquire the skill of hunting for food from the depths. As they become self-sufficient, their bodies become muscular, resembling men. A remarkable feature of their physical development is the growth of long fins on the back of their arms and calves. Additionally, a fin emerges at the posterior part of the mental lobe of their heads.

The Wobbaquas possess mesmerizing eyes that reflect a rainbow of colors, shimmering against the backdrop of their smooth gills. Their home lies deep beneath the ocean's surface, within domes that line the ocean floor, so remote that humans cannot reach them. When puberty arrives, many Wobbaquas venture out from their lifelong shelters, marking the beginning of the mating season for the younger individuals.

"Marriage isn't an endeavor for the faint-hearted. It's not always a state of eternal bliss. It encompasses the commitment to being there for each other through wealth, poverty, sickness, and health. These vows are taken for a reason! If your spouse remains your closest confidant, works tirelessly, and has stood by your side through both misfortunes and triumphs, through thick and thin, then be grateful that love has prevailed."

Emotions are vital for the Wobbaquas, and their hearts serve as the foundation that drives them. Picture two Wobbaquas beneath a waterfall, where oxygenated water cascades through a portal.

They bask in the sunlight that breaks the tranquility as it penetrates their gills, providing essential oxygen and hydration to their inner selves. By retracting their fins and smoothing their skin, they can transform into a human-like form.

The Wobbaquas possess a unique "soul spot" that cannot be hidden, as it represents their essence. However, they can wear clothing and present themselves as humans while maintaining a human-like appearance. They must keep their resemblance to humans in mind and occasionally shift their thoughts to remain in their human form. Without realizing it, they must continuously maintain this mindset, even though they may prefer to stay as they are. This can pose challenges when they come into direct contact with humans, as they must remain in their human form to navigate the human world. Despite this, deep down, they long to return to the water. Some Wobbaquas can stay out of water for more extended periods than others. They stand firm and resolute, fighting against the same battles as humans.

The transformation of the Wobbaquas has brought together Millennial Man and Thunder to identify those disguised as humans right in front of the Wobbaquas. The isopod beds are being depleted of their nutrients by the Wobbaquas, who use their contents as drugs and cause hallucinations in humans. On the other hand, humans can dive to astonishing depths of 3,843 feet in small, cylinder-shaped submarines. However, Wobbaquas can venture to those depths unharmed without needing a submarine to protect them. The pure Isopod dust harvested at these depths is the target of Millennial Man and Brick Thunder's pursuit.

"According to reports, most of the isopod dust is being harvested and cultivated in the Mariana Trench, approximately 250 miles from Guam in the Pacific Ocean. The distribution of the dust is handled by many Asian individuals on the West Coast, spanning from California to Mexico. We have observed the drug being transported at swift currents in the Sechelt Rapids in Columbia, Canada," they explained. "One must exercise caution, as some Wobbaquas become prey for the massive Lion's Mane jellyfish during their journey. These jellyfish possess a dome-shaped body and long tentacles, scientifically named Cyanea Capillata by researchers who have studied this colossal creature. People are advised to be aware of its existence and learn how to respond if they come into contact with its stinging tentacles." One a college professor taught us." Thunder said.

Triangle

Off the coast of the Bermuda Triangle, at a depth of 8,178 feet, resides the Swires snailfish. This tiny creature poses no threat but emits electrical currents into the surrounding water near its nest. Brick Thunder patiently awaits a signal to act after completing his preparations. Reviewing informative videos showcasing the most transparent oceanic waters, he remarked, "We must carefully choose our battlegrounds. Locations like the Silfra Fissure in Iceland, the Weddell Sea in Antarctica, the Blue Lake in New Zealand, and certain cenotes in Mexico appear to be more suitable for combat, should it come to that. The inevitable truth is that a battle will arise between these two worlds."

"Preferably, the battle should occur in the oceanic waters," he continued. "This would give humans a better chance of survival, and the subsequent repairs required for either civilization would be minimized." The group reached a consensus on this point. "We should avoid the Weddell Sea, as it is teeming with plankton and abundant marine life," added Millennial Man. "I had the opportunity to swim with many creatures in Murano Sound, Antarctica, a newly discovered deep ice cap. Divers from the upper world found it beneath the glaciers. In that environment, the seawater left no trace behind. Once enclosed within the crystal bluc icc, we managed to extricate ourselves from the frigid depths of an ice cave." The atmosphere grew silent until suddenly, the realization struck. "We're trapped!" exclaimed one of them.

They found themselves tightly confined, akin to sardines in a can, searching for a means of communication. They were situated outside the parameters of the ice-filled cavern, where the civilization had constructed buildings that appeared invisible when viewed horizontally, perhaps only discernible from a vertical angle. "Reality struck us suddenly, and a shivering fear coursed through my being unintentionally," one of them recounted. Then, as if by some stroke of fortune, they managed to free themselves, swimming vigorously through a concealed air-hole.

After emerging briefly to the surface of their intentions, they dived back into the waters, swimming through the light, airless ice that shimmered like a portal to eternity," the Millennial man recounted. "On the other side of the massive white glacier, we descended rapidly towards the water, plunging into the solubilized seawater. Now, that was a thrilling dive!" he continued.

"It's a true marvel that we possess such agility. Coming from the depths of the iceberg's bottom, we skydived to freedom," a Millennial man remarked with awe. "The reality is, both Millennial man and Orbital man share a unique trait. They occasionally breathe a mixture of 80% helium and 20% oxygen. This enables them to stay at lower depths on the seafloor for extended periods. The abundance of helium grants remarkable buoyancy, allowing them to navigate the water like sailfish. A battle requires ample water to execute our plans," the Millennial man explained.

"Speaking of which," Orbital man interjected, "you may have other plans, Thunder, but I believe the Java Trench in the Indian Ocean is worth considering. It reaches a depth of 22,825 feet and is home to the Dumbo Octopus. These creatures are only a foot long, and numerous individuals inhabit the waterways. They could serve as a food source, particularly for the aquatic soldiers as we carry out our mission. They feed on the large worms that reside on the seafloor of this expansive region."

"What do you think, Thunder?" Millennial man inquired, his heart racing as he braced himself for Thunder's response. "So, I see," Thunder replied, carefully considering the options. He glanced between the men and said, "By joining forces, this should become a straightforward action plan to extract these culprits from the isopod beds and free the world from addiction to the dust. I am furious at what this cunning group of thugs has done. It's a shameful situation for civilization, and I acknowledge the damage caused. Unfortunately, such accountability is lacking in many high-ranking individuals." Thunder spoke, casting a sidelong glance. "We must remember that these culprits are as cold-hearted as maggots, willing to kill for what they believe in," Thunder emphasized, his voice cutting through the air.

"I'll have to return to Bell's Island for some relaxation before everything unfolds. I don't want to lose my inspiration amidst all this," Thunder declared. They left the area, focusing on the two individuals and resuming their daily routines. The other investigators stood dumbfounded by the magnitude of the undertaking, wondering if they could survive it all. Amidst the uncertainty, a rare rose Nautilus conch shell caught their attention.

The immense conch shell reaches the size of a two-story building, providing refuge for many isopod workers and serving as a hiding spot for those fleeing from predators. Once the danger subsides, they venture back home. Amidst their discussions, questions arise, leading to murmurs and note exchanges as they try to disqualify alternative plans for the upcoming confrontation. They know that a single mistake could result in significant loss of life. Meanwhile, the drug cartel continues its daily operations, making pickups and drops while they strategize.

"We must remain diligent in this endeavor, gentlemen," one of the senior detectives asserts. "The isopod pickups for the next few months have already taken place, and the drug cartel hotspots have cooled down as the drugs are already on the streets."

Closing his laptop, Thunder returns his focus to the room where he stands at the command center. "Indeed, we should schedule the battle against them within the next couple of weeks," he declares. The millennial man expresses surprise, saying, "You know more than I anticipated, sir!" His eyes turn cold and dark, resembling flint rock. "I insist we handle this with greater discretion," he adds.

Thunder inhales sharply, taken aback by the Millennial man's audacity in openly expressing his concerns. With a stern gaze, the Millennial man steps away from his screen. He ends the Skype call, emphasizing the need to focus on the task instead of delving into unnecessary details before the battle commences.

Thunder listens to a conversation about a woman being booked into the county jail due to her drug addiction. As he eavesdrops, Thunder hopes to gather information about the drop-off point for the drug delivery. The woman expresses her desperate situation, mentioning her addiction to the pills and inability to afford bail or a ride home. She laments the damage caused by her addiction and how it has alienated her from friends and family.

Frank, the officer handling the booking, tries to engage the woman in understanding the reasons for her arrest. Thunder, shaken by her words, retreats to his soundproof office to contemplate following her to the drug pickup location. Using the intercom system, Thunder communicates with the desk officer to learn about the dust drop-off. He realizes that once the drugs hit the streets, it becomes challenging to trace their origin.

Returning to the scene, Thunder signals the officer to have the woman appear before the judge and sets a personal reconnaissance bond. This way, Thunder ensures that they can monitor her closely. He understands the importance of sign language in coordinating their actions without alerting those unaware of their plans.

Thunder watches the defendant from a distance in his office, closing the blinds for discretion. He communicates through sign language with his team, preparing the vehicles to follow the officer driving her away from the precinct. Brick, another officer, cautions against immediately locking her up, and a younger officer approaches Thunder, discussing the necessity of staying within the bounds of the law.

As Thunder's sign language plan unfolds, the defendant is released from the judge's chamber, and the paperwork for her release is completed. An undercover officer, driving an unmarked car, approaches the defendant and offers her a ride. She eagerly accepts, admiring the officer's raggedy Ford and carrying her belongings in a worn-out purse made of Chinese grass.

Once inside the car, the defendant attempts to proposition the undercover officer, who is taken aback by her forwardness. As they merge onto the interstate, the officer sternly warns her to remain silent and points to her nose, indicating that he knows about her drug use. Feeling intimidated, she complies and asks to be dropped off at the downtown soup kitchen, where she believes she can find another ride.

The officer accelerates, maneuvering through three corners until they arrive at the red-and-black sign of the soup kitchen. Thugs loiter on the sidewalk, scouting for potential drug buyers. They engage people, asking if they're "looking," which is code for seeking drugs. This tactic helps the dealers identify new users while regular customers are already known. Notably, cartel members occupy the front of the kitchen, anticipating anyone interested in purchasing their illicit substance.

These runners can be found on every downtown corner, catering to executives and blue-collar workers who believe drugs will increase their productivity and help them earn their paychecks faster.

The undercover officer, reflecting on the dire situation of drug addiction in the area, opens the car door for the defendant, offering her a ride. She points to a makeshift shelter made of a blue canvas tarp tied between two trash cans, mentioning that she will be staying nearby. The officer assures her that he will check on her later in the day, indicating that an interrogation from Inspector Thunder is imminent.

Upon driving away, the officer observes the dismal living conditions of the downtown area, with many individuals barely dressed and wearing clothes obtained from goodwill boxes. He contemplates the challenging nature of his work in such an environment and heads to his next destination, leaving behind the troubled scene.

Back at his office, Thunder examines the records of those involved in drug addiction. He realizes many have been trapped in a cycle of addiction and incarceration, running to familiar faces and environments for acceptance. He notes the alarming number of individuals still addicted despite spending significant time in the system. Their addiction has consumed their lives and stolen their time on Earth.

He also acknowledges their financial struggles, with their earnings going toward legal fees and staying out of jail. Thunder observes how the drug affects their health, causing dental decay and clogging their arteries. He laments the loss of hope among these individuals, who may resort to devastating actions, including suicide. Some may also meet tragic ends through accidents or deteriorate into elderly addicts residing in nursing homes, waiting for their final moments.

The grim reality of the drug epidemic weighs heavily on Thunder as he contemplates its profound impact on individuals' lives and the broader community. "Family falls by the wayside as time passes; they know what life is about. Know what this lifestyle has done to those who won't listen." On second thought,

"That is where I come in, I'd guess!" These people, once fingerprinted, are in the system for life. We will follow up while Inspector Thunder uncovers the drug cartel kingpins! Back to the drawing board when it comes to the ocean inhabitants. You, investigators, know what your job is designed to accomplish.

Gather and identify every aspect of this investigation. I'll do the same.

Millennial's words about the beauty and vulnerability of mermaids catch Thunder's attention. Still, he is startled when he realizes that his microphone inadvertently broadcasts their conversation. Millennial expresses his concern for the safety of mermaids, particularly the Wobbaquas, who possess both aquatic and human qualities. He mentions how he enjoys observing them sunning on the beach or swimming together beneath the ocean.

Thunder, recognizing the significance of protecting these enchanting creatures, expresses his sadness over the instances where mermaids have been harmed by passing ships and boats due to their lack of awareness. He acknowledges the innocence and nurturing nature of the mermaids, emphasizing the importance of safeguarding them at any cost.

Upon hearing Millennial's thoughts about the potential need for a war to free the trapped isopod young ones in the depths, Thunder realizes the gravity of the situation. He understands that using slave labor is unacceptable and acknowledges the necessity of gathering supplies and planning for such a conflict should it arise.

The conversation steers their focus toward the dire situation faced by the mermaids and their determination to protect them, reflecting their shared commitment to preserving the innocence and well-being of these magical beings.

Chapter Six

Falling in Love

Rising to the oceanic surface, hearing thunder in the distance, the millennial man glides through the water like a wet noodle, navigating toward the source of the sound beyond the thunder.

A woman's voice slithers through the sound waves in the water. Is she looking out of curiosity? The millennial swims towards the lighthouse, located on the farthest banks of the Sugarmill Plantation, just off the coast of South Carolina. He hopes to catch a glimpse of the beautiful and pulchritudinous woman. As he approaches, he sees a human singing and wearing a bleak expression, gazing at the rushing waves brought ashore by the storm.

"Beauty beyond comparison is what she is, a streak of lean." He thought.

She stood beside the huge boulders at the foot of a cliff while the Millennial man watched her singing beautifully. The sound pierces his ears; he knows she is singing from the heart. She awaits her true love, who is supposed to arrive from the sea. The words to the melody she is singing are on a freighter, piercing his heart as her words penetrate his being. He feels what she feels, a longing too sad to identify. Deep loneliness fills his soul, and he experiences profound compassion as she sings of lost love.

Her white, invisible cotton dress catches his attention. Then a dusty, dark, reflective light from the lighthouse beams across the waters, and she does not stop singing. Awe-struck Millennial is standing upon the water's surface with his gape mouth, looking at her beauty. "I must know this one human he professes."

Coming to the edge of the dusty, dark cliff, he listens to her voice penetrating his heart. He longs to meet her, but he understands that, for now, he must remain incognito. Never do anything to hinder the investigation.

"Flashes of things going on in the Wobbaqua world come to mind."

"Should news of another world of sea creatures become a family name around the world? This might hinder the investigation."

"Therefore, sending many to look at the seaside for anything that looks like a sea creature?"

"No, I have to refrain from this."

The millennial man proclaimed and turned away. Slipping slowly and quietly beneath the oceanic surface, like a slice of ice, he disappears into the deep, watching as many Wobbaquas ride the dolphins. He was thinking while swimming around the Millennial wonders of his love.

"Only to return to this beautiful woman in the see-through dress night after night. One that adorns her natural closures," he thought. "I know I must keep her at arm's length."

"Should I especially prefer her in my life?" Millennial thought.

"My heart is bursting to know this beauty from a distance, he thought."

"My heart hurts when I think of what we could be, yet the deep separation of our hearts! Besides, the soul spot will be a factor in me being with her romantically."

My second thought is coming from the water. "Her singing is so pleasing to me." Stepping upon a nole, he stands so she can get used to his presence while she sings. She was looking at him and wondering what had him at the lighthouse night after night.

She thought. “What is he doing?”

Singing to her heart’s content, her want for the Millennial Man strides up. Each night, he steps a few steps closer to see her. She, in return, steps closer to the railing outside the lighthouse. There at the base of the cliff. One night, while singing, Millennial steps before her. His gaze locked in on hers! Lightning flowed from them both at such a visual connection.

After emerging from the seawater, she stops to gaze at the handsome man despite his wet and naked state. A Wobbaqua male can dry off, but he needs to be prepared to put on some clothes. Taking her scarf from her hand, the millennial wraps it around himself to cover his soul spot, reminding himself that he is human in front of her. Immersed in her presence, he forgets momentarily and instantly returns to his Wobbaqua form. She turns her head away, but seconds later, he propels himself towards her, transforming back into human form. He heads straight for her lips, and to his surprise, she remains still, not resisting or pulling away. A long and lingering embrace ensues, accompanied by the intense sensation from their kiss.

As he holds the lonely woman, he senses her tender emotions of prolonged solitude. "You knew what you were, yet you revealed yourself to me," she whispers. "I must ask you to keep our encounter discreet. I don't belong to the world as you know it." Startled, she expresses her agreement with a nod. With eyes wide and a yearning for this man, she edges closer to get a better look at him. There's an undeniable urge within her to reach out and caress his exquisite body as the concept of time loses its relevance.

Reaching out, he takes her hand and steps up over the railing of the mansion's seawall. He stands before her, encircling her entire body with his long arms in a deep embrace. As the pale moonlight envelops them both, he speaks romantically and softly. "You can experience this as often as you desire, but we must remain discreet." Peering deep into her soul telepathically, he understands she keeps her relationships hidden from her family.

The longing for the return of her lover from the sea can endure for an extended period. Millennial fills her heart and touches his soul spot, having delved into her mind and understanding the hunger within her for his passionate embrace. She senses his own need for companionship. His skin has transformed into that of a human, as he can switch between forms after emerging from the salty seawater. The cover of night conceals his nudity as he holds her warmly.

Stepping into the foyer of the vast plantation lobby, she contemplates sipping some sweet wine to relax. Quietly drifting towards her room, she stretches across an empty bed in eager anticipation, awaiting another rendezvous. The satin sheets beneath her already uncovered, heated body wrinkle. Upon closer inspection, she notices a small, iridescent fish scale on her arm, emitting fluorescent colors that captivate her attention. Marlina lifts the scale to the light, marveling at the wonder of her secret rendezvous.

Pulling her soft sheepskin pillow close with her arm under it, she sinks her face. “Was this a fish-man she has just had an encounter with?”

Rendezvous’ definition is - *a place appointed for assembling or meeting.*

As she listens to the wind rustling through the tall oak and hickory trees outside, Marlina drifts off to sleep, enveloped in pure satin softness. Leaving behind the noise of crickets and night sounds, he ventures out into the sea, heading towards his home drome. Slithering through the night waters, he relies on his radar to return to his abode. Once inside, he rinses off and settles onto his massive bed, rolling over to gaze at the dome's ceiling. The reflection of his brilliant-colored skin, adorned with fluorescent, multi-colored scales, captivates his attention.

However, he notices one scale missing, rubbing his long fingers across the vacant space. He recalls rubbing against the beauty by the sea, wondering if she may have the missing scale on her, hoping it will dissipate before she steps into direct sunlight, as it could blind her. Assured that she likely showered before bedtime, he felt a certain magic in her touch as he sensed their connection in her soul. "We will be one someday," he thought, gazing into the silence of his empty bedroom. Soon, he falls into a deep slumber, drifting through his dream world, reminiscing about the beauty and imagining his life with her.

Throughout the night, he tosses and turns in anticipation of being with her again. As the night passes and his dream world dissipates, he awakens to find crumpled sheets and sweat stains on his mattress. Wobbaquas all look the same except for Millennial men, as their skin differs.

"Falling in love only happens once in a lifetime," Millennial remarks. "Breeding is different; it merely tugs at the body, while true love tugs at the heart and emotions. It is an indescribable commitment between two individuals."

"My love for this songbird who frequents the archway by the sea has my undivided attention for now," he reflects.

It's amazing how being in love makes the other person appear so special.

"What will she do when she finally sees my true self? Then, perhaps, my appearance may be as insignificant as cheese grease," Millennial muses.

"I have spoken to her from the edge of the walkway, and we share deep feelings for one another," he mumbles slowly.

Transforming into the fish he is, he departs from his dome. He plunges into the sea, heading towards a scheduled meeting with his counterpart, Orbital Man. Swimming towards the pyramidal temples, the Millennial observes the city from the upper portion of the massive dome sky.

However, upon not finding the individuals he is supposed to meet, Millennial ventures into the open waters, swimming at the speed of sound across the ocean. He watches the activity of a school of whales, recalling the scientific studies facilitated by the professors at Philiff University of underwater technology and the finest laboratory on Earth. Arriving at the lighthouse, he searches for his fair maiden, feeling his soul spot pulsate in anticipation. Frustrated by his inability to locate her, he finds only an empty place by the sea's edge, prompting him to return to his domes.

"She knew I was watching her at the edge of the cliff. She knew I emerged from the ocean and had some knowledge of my appearance," he reflects.

"Though physical contact with her seems unlikely, should it ever become a reality, it would bring me immense joy to love her. One encounter is not enough for me. The time with her will come, and we will both understand from our souls what the future holds for us," he mutters while speaking to himself. "I want this woman to shake the foundation of my being!"

Capable of walking upon the surface of the sea, Millennial assumes his favorite formation, elevated telepathically three feet above the water's surface. Longings consume him as he yearns for this human connection, knowing deep down that it cannot work. Torn between returning to his domes or going back to the human who tugs at his heartstrings, he slides effortlessly into the shimmering embrace of the sea.

Like a knife through jello, he swiftly traverses the depths, returning to the domes. With little regard for anything else, his journey feels short and mentally drained; he finds solace in his home dome.

Meanwhile, his songbird by the sea wallows in her grief, reminiscing about her man who never returned from the sea. Night stretches on as Millennial prepares for the coming day, and in the stillness of his peaceful world, he dreams of a future with this woman. Yet, he realizes she must be his, and the longing intensifies. However, the night remains as lonely as the previous one. This phase in his life has propelled his emotions to new heights, and each day brings agony as he waits for love to grace his existence.

Despite this inner turmoil, Millennial takes his job seriously, repeating the same routine day after day, knowing in his soul spot that there is someone out there with whom he is meant to spend his life, beyond the realms of Orbital and the Father's existence. Peering into the abyss daily, Millennial senses that something is amiss in the aquatic world, something that could jeopardize the existence of his Wobbaquas. His entire world revolves around the safety and survival of the Wobbaqua civilization, warding off thoughts of an impending destructive force.

Swimming past the armory stations in the depths, he makes a mental note to be prepared should any disturbance in the seawater turn into a catastrophic event. Day after day, he watches and readies himself, passing through the area specifically designed for the production of weaponry. The inhabitants there are slightly different from the Wobbaquas, stringy and taller in stature. Many possess a warrior disposition, bearing the scars of countless battles. They stand prepared to fight, showing no mercy in a battlefield scenario. Observing from a distance, Millennial delves into their world mentally, deciphering the knowledge he seeks through his mystical vision. There is no need for questions, as his world has endowed him with the finest mental abilities in the universe.

Swimming swiftly past, Millennial realizes it's time to return to the seaside, where his woman awaits before she departs for the plantation. The aqua clock warns of stormy seas approaching the area, causing concern for the bomber stalls and gray structures. With a thought, he rests in his agile, fish-like body, swiftly navigating to the spot where he can watch her sing before sundown.

With a powerful thrust of his agile body, Millennial shoots high into the air, diving into the water with a splash and even deeper. He rises above the water's surface, beckoning her telepathically to join him in the water. She sings her heart out, and he mentally melts from longing for her. However, he knows he must not push or force her into his advances. He drops the thought, realizing that she must come to him willingly. His emotions have driven him to do foolish things. Now, he can listen to her singing and wait for the opportune moment to meet her without scaring her away from the walkway leading to the watchtower. Each turn of the lighthouse beams brings a glimpse of her beauty. Watching a burning love welling up inside him, he keeps his distance from the shoreline, listening from the darkness. As she turns and walks toward her bedroom at the end of the walkway and the edge of the plantation, Millennial swims into the depths. Home is essential in his world, and he must rest.

Glancing over his shoulder, he sees the mermaids swiftly turning and waving, expressing their gratitude for his time spent guarding their home. The journey back home has been long and exhausting. Millennial arrives at the city's depths, greeted by the sight of the deep blue massive structured domes. Weary from his quick journey, he enters his home dome to find some much-needed rest, transforming into his aquatic form. Millennial lies naked in his bed, covered with a sheet, reminiscing about his newfound and only love. Drifting off into a peaceful slumber, his mind filled with fantasies of Marlina.

As his eyes open, coming from a restful sleep, Millennial witnesses the sunrise in the deep. Looking up through the translucent dome, he observes nude mermaids swimming above the domes. Curious about their activities, he watches them emerge from the deep blue water. Their skin appears thin, tiny, and scaly, with a light pink hue. Some emit an aqua glow, while others occasionally flip out their fins. Many carry their offspring or nourish them until a certain age, holding them close to their breasts as they swim. As mermaids have their young Wobbaquas at their breasts, Millennial yearns for this experience with their mate. However, he recognizes the potential complexities of a relationship between a human and an underwater android, realizing the challenges beneath it all while lost in thought.

"I long to bring her to my dome, to immerse ourselves in warm water and bathe together. We would indulge in a massive open tub structure, with maids gently drizzling warm bath water over us. As we wallow in love and affection for each other, I want to ensure that every inch of her is dry, from head to toe. I would lovingly rub her body with warm oil and the sweet nectar of seabed flowers. She is a mature woman, ripe and soaked in desire.

I yearn to lie beside her on a dry, kelp bed, feeling her skin's smoothness against mine. And amidst it all, I want to caress the luxurious sixteen-hundred-count sheets as I feel her warm breath on my back. I want her to experience the love that fills me up, to know that it belongs to her if she reaches out for it. That is what I desire, although what I ultimately receive may be entirely different," Millennial sighs, acknowledging the uncertainty of his desires.

He recalls swimming back to the dome, realizing twenty mermaids are following him. They instinctively seek safety in numbers and carry their young ones attached to their breasts, each nurturing their offspring. They know he will guard and protect them on their journey, forming a bond of mutual trust and reliance.

"Some mermaids and others feed on surface fish while nursing

their young. These small fish are newly hatched and carry a hormone that aids in the growth of the babies' gills. Thus, they do not rely on their mothers for oxygen to survive the depths," Millennial ponders, observing the following mermaids. Opening his radar, he scans for any potential dangers in the waters between their current location and the city domes. Satisfied that there are no immediate threats, he leads them toward the gateway that leads to the nurturing mothers' colonies, noting the color of the water as a sign of safety.

"No one outside the domes is safe at this distance from safety, anyway," he acknowledges. Sharks are attracted to the green color of the water that brings them here. "I will address this situation once we reach the city," Millennial decides, thinking of the ones in the domes who miss him greatly. His new day will come soon, but it's time to rest. Retreating to his serene bedroom, he lies in the stillness of his dome, observing the fish and crabs moving above his bed upon the dome glass. Yet, his mind continues to wander to thoughts of this captivating beauty.

"How will she adapt to my surroundings? How could I adapt to hers?" he contemplates. Finding solace in rest, he believes that everything will fall into place. Questions persist, but his inner longing to be with her remains strong. Gazing up through the translucent pale blue dome, Millennial watches as the Nude top mermaids swim and observe their activities. Emerging from the deep blue water, their skin appears delicate and light pink, with occasional aqua glows in their fins. Many carry their offspring close to their breasts as they swim, mirroring how mermaids nurture their young. Millennial desires this experience for himself and his mate.

The mermaids express gratitude for his assistance in guiding them back to the domes after their long swim. He nods in acknowledgment and appreciation as they vanish into the blue water, appearing and disappearing like the ghosts of the sea. Although they are regarded as imaginary creatures, their presence is clear and iridescent. Some believe they are the spirits of those lost at sea, including sailors and those who drowned in these depths. "Life is sometimes like a decaying edge of a building foundation, slowly weathered by time. The old humans squander," Millennial remarks, swimming across the open depths and observing the rocky formations. He realizes that there is a greater danger to the Wobbaqua society than he initially thought, bringing a new sense of concern to his mind.

Chapter Seven

Heart-Wrenching

While observing the Wobbaqua workers harvesting the iso-pod beds, the Millennial man is taken aback by the enormity of the undertaking. The fact that these isopods serve as the primary food source for the Wobbaquas' society should suffice as a cause for concern.

"This could become a disaster if the supply and demand get out of balance," the Millennial man thought. The word "kilter" refers to a state of balance or working well, but it is typically used in the phrase "out of kilter."

"There was a stunning sunrise this morning. I rarely miss the opportunity to witness a sunrise as it symbolizes new beginnings and fresh starts in people's lives. We never know how many sunrises we will be blessed with, so I try to savor each one. I decided to engage in life a few years ago rather than merely exist actively. Remember, there is always a tomorrow! I hope the sun will rise in a peaceful world, free from all the hatred and anger that plagues it. It may seem like an impossible task, but deep down, people possess the capacity to understand that our current path is unsustainable. Therefore, let's cherish the present, express gratitude daily, and appreciate the little things that enrich our lives. Let's simply do our best," the Millennial expressed.

Many workers are not only drawn to the beds for harvesting but also to consume them as food. For the Wobbaquas, the beds are not a source of euphoric drugs; they are essential for sustenance. Consequently, numerous workers eat from their beds before starting their work shifts. These workers spend extended periods in the iso-pod fields, resulting in exhaustion and torn clothing due to the small legs of the isopods catching on the fabric. Some workers must search for new dresses while they continue their labor. Although distraught and aware that their involvement in harvesting illegal drugs will lead to their demise, they dutifully persist in loading open train cars with seeded isopods.

For some, this work provides a means of living, but many are enslaved to the cartel. In the past, most isopods were transported through waterways, alongside large shipping freighters, to be delivered to New York Harbor near Manhattan. From there, they were transferred onto smaller boats and taken to distillate island drops for sorting by humans, who would then produce drugs. Finally, the drugs were transported to the mainland.

The illegal distribution of drugs to unsuspecting individuals brings Brick Thunder into the scene, deeply troubled by this deceitful operation. This drug is a menace, especially to the young people in society, and even those in the Wobbaqua world have fallen victim to its addictive grip. Many of them are coerced into labor by oppressive overseers who force them to toil in the Wobbaqua fields, leaving them torn, dejected, and separated from their families. The mafia preys on their vulnerability, making them victims of these dire circumstances. Amidst the mines, the workers silently yearn for liberation from this wretched existence. Rumors circulate that the Millennial is coming to their rescue. Still, mounting doubts result in many being confined to prison cells deep within the mines, ensuring obedience and suppressing resistance. The environment is suffocating, with scarce oxygen for survival. Reality strikes and the Millennial realizes this situation could spell our doom.

Seeking a means of transportation, the Millennial ventures towards a car portal and steps into a pod—a structure that carries individuals to specific destinations. These pods are strategically placed near the mines, capturing intruders and serving the needs of those seeking a particular location, even if it involves swimming past a school of whales or navigating shark-infested waters without risking their lives. Pod travel is widespread within the domes, encompassing miles of underwater routes, providing convenient access for frequent travelers. Observing the abhorrent circumstances, a Millennial man is overcome with despair.

The Millennial is determined to end this exploitation, particularly by confronting those responsible for robbing the Wobbaquas of their livelihood. The more abusive the Wobbaqua drug cartel becomes, the more they believe pushing the weaker ones toward extinction is acceptable. Some rebels attempt to fight back, only to be cast into a pitch-black underwater cavern, left waiting until someone remembers their captivity. Like scavengers devouring a two-day-old KFC, they persist until nothing remains.

The gravity of the situation is evident. "One woman, in particular, possesses remarkable dynamism, abundant energy, and creative thinking. Unfortunately, she fell into the trap of isopod dust addiction. She finds an older man or woman to support her habit, extracting money from them to obtain the dust regularly. This destroys their ambition," Thunder lamented.

"She provides them with the dust to sustain her addiction, manipulating her partner's finances through a proxy, exploiting the husband through his wife. Such circumstances are common among those ensnared by isopod dust. Those who exploit others in this manner are held in high regard by their enablers, moving through their social circles with a constant codependent presence."

Similar to the small fish that trail behind a whale, those addicted to isopod dust take advantage of anything the whale doesn't need or use. This leaves their close families suffering from the loss of a husband or wife, drained by the individual who feeds off them. Unfortunately, this behavior is common among those trapped in isopod dust addiction. One must observe behavioral changes, as they often indicate whether a family member or friend is under the influence of the dust. They tend to isolate themselves from their loved ones to continue their pursuit of the substance.

Family peace projects provide food and shelter for those attempting to break free from the clutches of addiction. It's a distressing situation for everyone involved, with so much hatred. Many show compassion towards these individuals, aware they will likely end up begging or panhandling on street corners daily to sustain their fix. Numerous addicts wander the streets, functioning but lost. "Lost ones," he sighed, shaking his head.

"The workers in the isopod beds are in even worse condition. He explained that many are covered in white spots, indicative of ICK, a disease commonly found in freshwater fish," he explained. Saltwater Wobbaquas are usually less susceptible to this disease. There are colonies of ICK, where the white spots become so severe that they trail behind the infected individuals as they move through the water, clinging to their scales. Those heavily infested are often migrant workers who have infiltrated the colonies. Many were transported after being caught in ICK camps, only to be returned to the ocean's depths, where the ICK colonies attempted to restore their health.

Leopard disease is another prevalent skin disease in these migration times between colonies. Many refer to the protrusions on the skin as ICK. Compassionate Wobbaquas in the colonies provide massive acres of soaping holes on the city's outskirts. These holes, resembling adult-sized pits in the ground, have small motors attached to make them efficient. A piece of sea glass, akin to a coin, is required to operate the motors. Various types of soap are available to remove barnacles, an arthropod belonging to the infraclass Cirripedia in the subphylum Crustacea. Barnacles exclusively inhabit marine environments and tend to attach themselves to the outer surfaces of deep-sea inhabitants, particularly crabs and lobsters. Many individuals travel for miles to have their barnacles removed using the grinder rocks lining the soaping holes. These formations span acres of seabed, with each community having at least one. The path leading to the soaping holes is illuminated by the vibrant lights of the coconut octopus, displaying iridescent rainbow colors with a leading luminosity that can be seen from space. The soaping holes closer to the city excel at removing stubborn, encrusted barnacles often found on the elder Wobbaquas.

Better equipment is stationed near the city, and trucks regularly collect the scales and debris left behind during the barnacle removal process. City enforcement codes ensure swift disposal of the debris, which is then repurposed to build homes for individuals in need within the local civilizations. Bud, a Wobbaqua, chimed in, "This alone creates jobs." Some individuals choose to remain and work in the area after getting clean.

A Wobbaqua with a crustacean covering their entire face and body steps inside the scrub pods designed to envelop anybody. Like a sea worm vanishing into the sandy ocean floor, those entering the scrub pods undergo a similar transformation.

Emerging, clean, and invigorated, this ongoing business venture has proven profitable for many. After scrubbing, individuals proceed to a fogger room, where they are misted with oils and powdered before returning to the water world they are accustomed to.

The pervasive odor emanating from the fish is quite overwhelming. Before entering the city, they must visit the soaping holes—it's a legal requirement, as Millennial explains. "Inmates from the county and city jails are brought out after hours to clean the soaping holes owned by the city," he elaborates. These jail inmates, designated as trustees by the sheriff, are entrusted with specific tasks inside the jail premises and are now permitted to work outside the jail, usually in county government buildings or other public facilities, always under the supervision of a corrections officer or deputy sheriff.

"Many inmates are reluctant to perform this task due to the lice infestation in the city-owned holes. The lice cling to anyone who enters, causing intense itching that provides no respite within the confines of a jail cell. When the soaping holes are illuminated by ultraviolet light, their visibility extends for miles. Still, in the depths, it feels as if you're on a never-ending treadmill. It's a different experience than what humans typically encounter. The soaping holes offer a welcoming escape for many to cleanse themselves. They are open to the public, emanating delightful scents of aromatic perfumes, soaps, and powders. Upon entering the domes, one is greeted by a pleasant tropical aroma, especially in the areas with finer amenities," he explains.

As individuals emerge from the soaping holes, those arriving can't help but take in the aromatic ambiance surrounding them—makeup, powders, perfumes, and vibrant wraps, particularly appealing to female and male individuals with distinctive fashion preferences. However, some exhibit a distinct look of anguish. Water-worthy vehicles are sold to those who appreciate unique designs, catering to their needs. Several waterborne creatures, especially the fourth-generation ones, utilize the soaping holes to remove roughage and kelp from their skin, often developing a hereditary crustacean of sea moss.

"Buckle-backs, known for their shimmering shellbacks, also frequent the soaping holes. They relish being buffed to a sparkling shine, resulting in colonies of buckle-backs residing nearby," he shares, adopting the demeanor of a public speaker. Millennials describe the history of the soaping holes and their community benefits. "Many question the advantages of soaping holes for the public. Without these meticulously maintained holes, we would witness a higher prevalence of diseases within the community, increased crustation littering the sidewalks and public spaces, and impeding public access. Sanitation is another crucial factor," he continues. "These soaping holes effectively eliminate numerous microorganisms in the seawater, purifying the frequently used areas, contributing to public health and well-being."

He then offers an example to illustrate what one can expect when the soaping holes are used—the octopus's response when angered.

Octopuses are indeed territorial creatures, but it's important to note that they generally do not go after humans unless they feel threatened or provoked. In such cases, they may exhibit defensive behavior, potentially leading to an attack. Observing the unhappy appearance of the octopus in the given context, it would be wise for the diver to exercise caution and retreat to a safer distance.

Great white sharks are indeed apex predators with remarkable hunting abilities. Their powerful swimming capabilities enable them to breach the water's surface, propelling themselves nearly 11 feet in the air. While witnessing their hunting prowess may be fascinating and awe-inspiring, it is certainly not an experience one would desire as their prey.

When it comes to the battle between humans and these predators of the deep, humans must have a comprehensive understanding of the intricacies of these species.

This knowledge is necessary to navigate and coexist with them, as humans could inadvertently become part of their food chain in certain circumstances.

The mysterious creature that combines elements of an eel and a leopard seal is a cute and cuddly mammal that we adore seeing pictures of. Imagining their adorable babies brings joy to our hearts.

Moving on to the Buckle Back, they form a colony that emerged from the ocean's depths. Many reside beneath the kelp beds in hollowed-out caves and caverns that have developed over centuries. Beneath it lies the aquifer, a body of saturated rock through which water can easily flow. Aquifers must possess permeability and porosity and can include rock types like sandstone, conglomerate, fractured limestone, and unconsolidated sand and gravel. Fractured volcanic rocks and rubble zones between volcanic flows also make excellent aquifers. To access the water, a well must be drilled into an aquifer. Rocks like granite and schist generally have low porosity and thus make poor aquifers unless they are heavily fractured. In that case, they can still serve as good aquifers. A well is a hole drilled into the ground to reach an aquifer; typically, water from a well must be pumped to the surface. Suppose water is pumped from a well faster than it is replenished. In that case, the water table can be lowered, potentially causing the well to dry.

When water is pumped from a well, the water table is often lowered into a cone of depression centered around the well. Groundwater typically flows downhill towards the well along the slope of the water table. Freshwater meets seawater in the bu-depths beneath the sea, creating a line of demarcation. Buckle Backs can traverse between both regions, but they must return to seawater content within three hours, or they may undergo mental deterioration. Buckle Backs are hardworking creatures with a strong focus on completing tasks. They possess an excellent work ethic, making them perfect candidates for various jobs. Millennial individuals appreciate their attitude towards the depths and their ability to maintain peace among colonies. Many Buckle Backs diligently show care in their duties, and this dedication makes a significant difference in their world.

These octopuses earned their name from the Wobbaquas due to the pack-like structure on their backs that resembles a buckle. With a back resembling a tortoiseshell and a turtle-like face, many of them are covered in barnacles of different colors. They form colonies to assist the Wobbaquas in any way they deem necessary.

No entity, whether Wobbaquas, Millennials, or orbitals in the depths, dominates the Buckle Backs. Due to colonization, they have also survived in the kelp beds. Buckle Backs have fins for feet, enabling them to walk, and some feed on shells while others collect sea glass. They possess unique adaptations that help them thrive in the ocean's depths.

Due to their messy nature, they are not allowed inside the city or the domes; instead, they reside beneath the seafloor. If the war continued, thousands would come forward as an army to aid the Wobbaquas, serving as helpful neighbors. They carry walking sticks and swords made from various underwater materials and wear attire adorned with sparkling jewels.

Their vision is limited to black and white, enabling them to navigate the caverns they inhabit. Many stones retain light for extended periods, a crucial resource for illumination.

Any colony that offers assistance to the Wobbaquas is warmly welcomed, and they bring an abundance of equipment to the scrapyard, an area the size of two football fields. An adventurous older man with a knack for trying new things marvels at the vast array of items available to develop weapons. The enthusiastic old man shows excitement and interest in these endeavors.

Around five hundred Buckle Backs arrive on small ocean-bearing wagons resembling miniature jeeps likely constructed from deep-sea remnants. Many pull trailers are made of mesh crafted from hollowed coral and stone wheels. These trailers are heavily loaded with supplies, causing the seabed to be churned up, resulting in sand swirling in the water. The wagons are equipped with flashing lights to indicate their whereabouts, and the Buckle Backs wear distinctive flapped hats, some in plaid, with earpieces sticking out.

Their unique fashion sense includes tight-fitting hats, and they wear binocular-like vision apparatus, which they receive as babies to combat water blindness. Despite their peculiar appearance, Millennial individuals and the old man stand observing them, recognizing the goodness in their hearts. The inventive old man can imagine and create new things while displaying sympathy and caring for others' problems.

Seahorses, sea snakes, and other sea species watch from the sidelines as each vehicle arrives with supplies. They gather, wondering what is stirring up so much sand from the ocean floor.

Among the vehicles brought by the Buckle Backs, many are crafted from remnants of the sea. Some even include man-made items like a pastel blue 1950 Buick automobile adorned with extensive chrome detailing. Over the years, numerous Fords have been discarded from ships during supply trips from China, as some were painted with iridescent colors to make a striking impression. These vehicles were thrown overboard because foreign governments were prohibited from operating factories and buying or selling products on American soil.

Feeling intimidated, the Asian governments disposed of the goods and migrated to America, establishing partnerships with sovereign companies that manufactured products approved by the government before being shipped.

Gaining recognition is crucial for the Buckle Backs as they strive to prove their worth to the Wobbaqua world. They consider it a privilege to contribute to the cause. Meanwhile, the children who accompanied their parents are left by the side of the road to be picked up later, as the Millennial emphasized that no children are allowed inside the dome housing the weaponry. This precaution ensures faster progress and enhances safety. Cheering from the sidelines, the children wave at each passing vehicle, which carries heavy truck beds filled with metal and equipment.

Some Buckle Backs have welders, acetylene and cutting torches, and oxygen tanks stored near the cab of their underwater vehicles. One child, Buckle Back, excitedly waves and asks his brother, "Look, Sonny, look at all this!"

"I understand, my brother. We are living in a time where everything can change in the blink of an eye," the gregarious Buckle Back responds, thoroughly enjoying the company of others. "We have to follow Daddy's instructions and wait here for his return," he adds. These two adventurous young Buckle Backs have a penchant for trying new things.

With great enthusiasm and interest, they eagerly anticipate the opportunity to visit the soaping holes, as they are always looking for potential romantic partners. "Yes! I saw Daddy mark the mile marker to the city on his wrist, so he will know where to return to amidst all this commotion in the water," one of them exclaims. "Well, what mile marker are we at?" the other asks. "Looks like 1313 to me!" he responds.

Observing the vehicles loaded with precision, they recognize the telltale signs of individuals with a military background. "It's evident that they received training that instilled a passionate approach to executing tasks. Regardless of gender, they believe in the importance of their work and their emotional well-being hinges on its success," the older Buckle Back remarks.

Positioned atop a tall bank beside the roadway, they watch the procession as it enters the city, enjoying an excellent view. They are accompanied by other young Buckle Backs who were also left behind, with the older ones taking responsibility for their younger counterparts. Daddy is a kind and considerate figure, always thinking about the welfare and emotions of others.

Once the caravan unloads inside the domes, the vehicles turn around and leave the area. They are headed to pick up their offspring and return to the caverns where the Buckle Back society resides.

Many in the procession emerged from the murky water, their lights flashing as they hurriedly made their way along the roadway. "Look!" they exclaimed, marveling at the courageous individuals who seemed to materialize from the mountainside. These unique beings could transform themselves to adapt to rough surfaces and take on irregular shapes. They were known for their eccentric nature and preferred keeping to themselves unless Millennials required assistance.

As the beautifully illuminated lights appeared and vanished in the cloudy water, Millennial observed, "Courageous is an understatement for our Daddy! He's the coolest dad ever!" They scooted closer to the cliff's edge, filled with excitement and awe. "This is the biggest thing in our lives right now!" one exclaimed.

"Look! Daddy is coming for us!" they shouted with joy. "Come on, let's stand close to the roadway." One of them pulled out a small shell-shaped cell phone and asked, "Are you calling Daddy?"

"He told us only to use the phone in case of an emergency," the other responded.

"But we need to know his estimated time of arrival. It can get risky standing so close with so much activity," the young Buckle Back insisted.

"You're right, go ahead and make the call," the other agreed. The young Buckle Back dialed the number and walked down the slope toward the roadway. "The visibility is poor, and we should stay close to each other. I can't afford to lose you in all this," he said.

"Daddy! When will you be picking us up?" he asked eagerly over the phone.

"On my way, son. The water is murky, making navigating challenging," Daddy reassured them. "Come on, Daddy; we'll be waiting at the mile marker you specified," the Buckle Back replied.

"Sure enough, son! I'm about two minutes away," Daddy confirmed.

"We better hurry!" the young Buckle Back exclaimed, putting the flip phone back into his pocket. They quickly made their way to the designated mile marker.

With everything settled, Millennial and Ol' Man emerged from the murky water, spitting out the sand. "The stifling sand makes it hard to breathe," Millennial remarked. All the Wobbaquas left the area to save themselves from going home sick due to the lack of oxygen needed to survive. Just as they were about to leave, a blast was heard.

"Suddenly, the ocean churned, extending to the center of the vortex of the abyss. Then, it exploded with oxygenated water, surrounding the Wobbaquas on their way home," Millennial described the miraculous scene.

This incredible phenomenon resulted from Daddy's telepathic connection with Millennial and his crew, a thought that became a reality. It provided the much-needed oxygenated water and washed away the black suit from the depths. They drifted out of sight, leaving the other swimmers at the site to accomplish their mission.

"Let's leave them to do what they set out to accomplish," Millennial suggested as they swam through the sea depths. With a nod, Ol' man, showing his long tail, disappeared into the depths. Together with the other Wobbaqua warriors, they returned to the domes in the massive oxygenated water. "He notices a shipwreck from the pirate era called Blackbeard. He wants to explore it and sees massive cannons covered in barnacles and crustaceans. He knows there is still some good left in them," Millennial thought.

Leaving the rest behind, Millennial and Ol' Man swam outside the domes and circled the wreckage. Startling a few fish sheltered in the hull, they marveled at the white skulls and bones of those who perished in the wreckage. Millennial signaled a few Wobbaquas to dismantle the ship and collect anything to aid their underwater war. Telepathically, he explained the purpose and turned to Ol' Man, signaling him to return to the oxygenated water. Darkening around his eyes and gills turning deep purple from the lack of oxygen, Millennial urged Ol' man to hurry.

With a rush of water before his face, Millennial absorbed the much-needed churning oxygenated water to survive and regain his strength. He reached out to Ol' Man, and they emerged from the depths near the dilapidated shipwreck, returning to where they had first seen it. Many Wobbaqua warriors escorted them back to the domes, where they could finally rest. Tired and worn out, Ol' Man nibbled on water chestnuts and coral cookies before slipping into a slumber. Millennial, still gazing at the moonbeams entering his dome, thought, "It has been a long day. I love Millennial!" As his gills closed, he curled into a small ball, wrapping his tail around his head and blending into the rock bed.

Millennial slipped away to listen to his songbird at the lighthouse before venturing into the open water, swimming through the lavender-colored moonbeams. However, as he swam, he encountered a crab fishing vessel anchored nearby. The ship had dropped numerous crab cages, and Millennial found himself entangled in a mass of ropes as a storm brewed. Realizing the danger, he pulled out a sharp knife and began cutting the ropes, leaving the cages loose on the ocean floor.

Navigating through the churning water, he finally escaped the entanglement. Before him, the ocean opened up, and he disappeared into the depths, swimming as fast as a speeding bullet. Eventually, he reached the shoreline near the lighthouse, where Marlina awaited him. As she stood close to the water's edge, he transformed from his sea body into his human-like form. They embraced, and Marlina sang a soft lullaby, melting Millennial's heart.

They sat together on a park bench beside the dunes, enjoying each other's company. Millennial shared his master plan to clear the depths and help humanity, leaving Marlina in awe and filled with love for this extraordinary man. She was captivated by his sweet spirit and soul. Millennial revealed that his love for her was beyond measure.

As they wrapped their arms around each other, Millennial and Marlina discussed their shared vision. They marveled at the beauty of the domes at sunset, with moonbeams shooting blue-violet beams through the churning water. Soft lavender and maroon lights illuminated the seabed, creating a tranquil atmosphere as the Wobbaqua world prepared to rest for the night.

Millennial and Marlina returned home to the domes, crossing the massive entrance to the city and several smaller domes along the way. As they entered their controlled water world, they felt the perfect oxygen levels adjusting to their fins. The comfort zone was reached, and they savored the serene atmosphere. Exhausted from the day's events, Ol' man found solace in his bed, nibbling on water chestnuts and coral cookies before slipping into a deep slumber.

Millennial, still moved by the moonbeams, swam towards his resting place, reflecting on the day's events. He thought about the adventure that awaited him in the depths, eager to continue his journey. As he drifted to sleep, he felt a sense of fulfillment and anticipation for the challenges and wonders ahead.

Roman aqueduct - Zaghouan, Tunisia

The Zaghouan aqueduct, constructed during Emperor Hadrian's reign in 122, was designed to transport water from Jebel Zaghouan to Carthage. This section of the aqueduct is located near Tunis. The aqueduct was a crucial water supply system for the ancient city, ensuring a steady water flow for various purposes.

In the ocean's depths, tunnels extend along the length of the Mariana Trench. Many Wobbaqua warriors have found their way into these tunnels, surviving for extended periods in the depths of the earth. They dwell alongside the volcanic waters that characterize the deepest parts of the abyss.

These tunnels provide a unique environment for the Wobbaqua warriors, offering challenges and resources. The volcanic activity in the vicinity creates a distinctive ecosystem with flora and fauna adapted to extreme conditions. The warriors have adapted to this environment, utilizing their skills and resilience to navigate and survive in the depths.

Exploring the tunnels of the Mariana Trench can be an arduous and perilous journey. However, for the Wobbaqua warriors, it offers an opportunity to expand their knowledge and understanding of the underwater world. They find hidden secrets within these depths and encounter unique species that have adapted to life in the darkness.

The tunnels of the Mariana Trench serve as a testament to the resilience and adaptability of life in the depths of the ocean. They are a mysterious and awe-inspiring realm that continues to fascinate and challenge those who venture into its depths.

Chapter Eight
The War of Both Worlds

The Scrapyard

The beauty of the sea captivates the Millennial man as he stands cool, calm, and collected, gazing across the vast expanse. Balanced on a massive boulder, he looks up at the sunbeams piercing the underwater realm, illuminating the kelp beds. He absorbs the splendor of the kelp beds and the deposits of the coral reefs, admiring the exquisite statues in the Philiffi city graveyard.

His thoughts dwell mostly on the current state of the Wobbaqua world, which has undergone a significant shift. Swimming from one beautiful location to another, the Millennial man sits beside the swelling ebb tide, patiently awaiting his return home. Throughout his journey, he ponders the implications of the ongoing war and how his strategies will come into play amidst the circumstances. Brick Thunder, a familiar name, comes to mind. Understanding the importance of knowing this man, he realizes that resolving the situation requires his acquaintance.

The war against the Wobbaquas' exploitation of the isopod beds persists, and the Millennial man considers the collective impact of this cleanup on the city dwellers and the dome communities beneath the oceanic waters. In the distance, the dolphins sense the danger emanating from his presence. They watch as a howling seal approaches him through the waters. He swiftly traverses the abyss with a spear, propelled by astronomical speeds.

His telepathic abilities allow him to sense those who will cross his path even before they arrive—a trait ingrained deep within him. As he reaches the salvage barns, which house remnants from the previous battle, he takes in the scene before him.

Observing as numerous Wobbaqua citizens and warriors unite, pooling their efforts to salvage whatever they can, the Millennial man carefully assesses the situation. He marvels at the power of collective action and wonders how such a concerted effort can make a significant impact. The main objective remains clear: to protect the water world from predators. Recognizing the crucial importance of their assistance, he witnesses their tear-filled eyes as they watch him swim across the barrier after opening the portal.

Regaining his focus, the Millennial man stands and gazes at the mystical world of the frozen ones. Their gratitude is expressed as they exclaim how greatly he has aided the Wobbaqua world. Flipping his head and propelling himself through the warm depths, he uses his fins to generate speed. Soon, he immerses himself in a meeting, reigniting the remaining resources to conclude the war against the isopod thieves. "We must salvage everything possible," he asserts.

"I have discovered a shipwreck containing cannons and a substantial supply of ammunition," he announces. "We can repurpose them into jet-propelled weapons to eliminate the remaining thieves who have corrupted the world we once knew." He explains that the ship was a battleship, claiming the lives of many humans when it sank. They must extract what they need while discarding the unnecessary remnants, leaving them in the depths. As he gazes across, he spots the realm of the frozen ones.

As the Millennial man remarked, individuals among the Wobbaquas have transformed into a native-like group known as the Indians. Many reside in the depths, within the oceanic waters, encompassing icebergs and glaciers. It's their home, akin to living in underwater igloos," Millennial explained.

"Their entire existence revolves around survival, particularly in extreme cold. They have developed the remarkable stamina to maneuver icebergs physically, placing them strategically to create a habitat for their civilization," Millennial continued, mentally visualizing the process with a slender wand on the drawing board.

"Millennial?" Orbital interjected, seeking clarification. "Perhaps they calculate the number of years they can sustain themselves on an iceberg before it melts and sinks into the unforgiving seawater," Orbital suggested.

"Millennial describes them as missing something," Orbital continued. "Who would willingly live in such conditions?" he pondered.

"They possess their formidable force, armed and ready! They offer their battle tactics to save the Wobbaqua world," The Millennial replied, astonished by their willingness to sacrifice their loved ones for the cause.

"Do you understand the importance of this cause?" Millennial inquired.

"Yes, what's happening in the Isopod fields is absurd. We must fight to free those trapped by these fools," Master Frozen declared, his words squeezed out as his cheeks froze in the tepid waters.

"Sir, I can see you're uncomfortable. I suggest you continue on your intended path and find more suitable water temperatures," Millennial advised, acknowledging Master Frozen's discomfort.

"Yes, you have adapted, and well... I still prefer the tropical atmosphere and home comfort," Master Frozen responded. Retrieving a frozen piece of sea glass from his chest pocket, he handed it to Millennial, his pale blue eyes meeting Millennial's gaze. The small blue sea glass served as a token of their exchange.

"Should you ever need me or my people, Millennial, just rub this," Frozen said, presenting the small blue sea glass. "Within a few minutes, we will be by your side, wherever you may be."

"Magic, huh?" Millennial questioned.

"Yes, you could say that," Frozen smiled. "My militia will be ready and waiting when you call upon us, Millennial. Remember that we will be coming from the North Pole, from the icy surface of the Earth."

"Make a mental note of those coordinates," Millennial instructed. "When you rub the blue sea glass, the coordinates will appear in the surrounding water. You can use that to your advantage."

Placing the tiny blue glass under a fin, Millennial realized he needed to escape the cold water. He glanced across the depths of the frozen slush, spotting lights emanating from the igloo-like structures. The beauty of the submerged city captivated him with its abundance of blue ice, miles of igloos, street lights, and intricately carved ice buildings.

Majestic statues commemorating those who had passed adorned the city of the frozen ones. Their pale blue skin glowed with fluorescence, reminiscent of the color of lightning bugs.

"It appears more advanced than I initially thought," Millennial observed as he surveyed the scene. "They possess an extra fin to navigate the slushy ice and reach their destinations. However, they are still true Wobbaquas!"

"Time is of the essence," Millennial sighed. "I must return to my city now and determine the remaining plans needed to initiate all this." Ascending above the glacier, the Millennial man swam swiftly toward warmer waters, eager to escape the cold temperatures. As he glanced back at the splendid waterways, shimmering with vibrant colors, he pondered the frozen ones' survival strategies and food harvesting methods. He had a few more questions, but the water's frigid temperature prevented him from dwelling on them comfortably.

The Shipwrecks

The old man recounted, "To my surprise, even the cannons were intact in the sunken ship. Blackbeard's crew's bravery led to its demise at the bottom of the sea. Hidden beneath the galleys, the crew made the approaching mariners believe the vessel was abandoned. As soon as the crew of the oncoming ship boarded, they emerged from beneath the galleys, taking them by surprise."

"Blood splattered across the ship's deck, drenching them in a bloody bath beneath the decks. The seawater ran red that day!" Millennial exclaimed, observing the old man hurriedly salvaging parts of the shipwreck for upcoming battle weaponry.

"There have been many lives lost on this vessel, with hollow human skulls still inside," Millennial mentioned solemnly. "Let us remember that these ships once housed human beings, and we pray that nothing hinders our efforts." He continued to observe, briefly describing the ship that had sunk, revealing that it was Blackbeard's last ship before his demise by the seaside.

Furthermore, the Queen's Ransom ship met its fate off the Caribbean coast," Millennial added. "It possesses numerous cannons that we can salvage to aid in weapon production. We should also search for swords on the seafloor, which can be repurposed. However, we must approach this with caution and use our judgment. Many shipwrecks are the final resting places for those lost due to human error and adverse weather conditions."

The Millennial emphasized respecting these shipwrecks as solemn graveyards for the deceased.

This indicates that we have the potential to overcome these challenges and reclaim our world as we have come to know it," Millennial asserted. With a wave of his hand, he opened his pointer finger and middle finger, projecting a screen-like image in front of everyone. The screen displayed the sunken ship, showcasing the armor and weaponry on board. Pointing to a hole in the ship's hull, he explained that it was the reason for its demise. On the side facing up, he indicated the location of the cannons and the numerous boxes of ammunition that could be salvaged.

"We can take these resources and transform them into advanced modern-day weapons using the technology in our god chamber, along with the pods we emerged from, returning to our birthright," Millennial elaborated. Closing his fingers, the image remained suspended in the watery air as a reference for future use. Sliding his fins across the floor, he swiftly moved forward, too pressed for time to secure them tightly against his calves. However, due to the moisture change in the water surrounding everyone, they retracted on their own after a few seconds.

A Millennial approached one of the older workers, seeking a private conversation. "Sir, could I have a few minutes alone?" he requested. The elderly man, with weary eyes, nodded and replied, "Yes, of course."

"Come, let's step outside and discuss the project at hand," Millennial suggested. "I have discovered some crashed aircraft at the bottom of the cliff near the shore of Newfoundland. We can retrieve and repurpose them to create the necessary equipment to bring about the desired change in our world. Would that be of any help to the Mold foundry?"

Walking side by side, they moved towards the outdoor foyer of the ammunition scrap yard office. The Millennial Man, searching for a more private location, noticed a nearby pub. "Shall we go for a refreshing drink?" he proposed. "Perhaps Hasty, the server, can prepare us some turtle eggs and a slab of crab meat."

"Sure!" the old man agreed. They navigated through a maze of sound barriers, as sound carries differently in water, and proceeded down the street to enter the pub. Millennial released the sound barrier from the water with a swish of his hand, focusing his attention back on the conversation. They found a small table in a dimly lit corner and ordered their preferred drinks.

"I'll have a khaki-colored Frappe, generously topped with whipped cream and drizzled with caramel," the old man stated with a grin.

"A dry cool-aid for me," Millennial requested. As they engaged in conversation, Millennial wrapped his hand. It swung his arm, creating an invisible cover of silence around them within a privacy dome encompassing the table. It became apparent that the old man had spent his entire life working in the mold foundry, a factory that produced metal castings. His expertise in revamping weaponry was unparalleled, earning him great respect and honor.

The Ol' man's extensive knowledge of weapon modifications became evident at the table as the conversation unfolded. His clothing, worn and torn from years of wearing the same attire daily, showcased his dedication and experience.

The old man had lived on a modest budget from humble beginnings. His coral-strapped steel-toed shoes had thick soles to prevent metal pieces from piercing his feet. His worn gray lunchbox was slowly opened before him on the table, revealing a couple of lobster tails and some sea biscuits. The Millennial man observed the contents being unveiled, never ceasing his conversation as there was much to discuss.

"Leave this to me," the old man declared, taking a bite of the lobster tail and chewing. He extended a lobster tail towards the Millennial man, offering to share. "No, thank you, sir," the Millennial man responded telepathically, expressing his gratitude.

"I am honored to be working on this project," the old man said. "I have dedicated my life to this place, and whatever you need to be built, just let me know." Sitting across from the weathered old man, the Millennial man assessed the situation and presented his challenge to him.

"Sir, I will require you to create several weapons suitable for the underwater environment," the Millennial man conveyed. "They should also be adaptable for use in the world above water." He spoke softly through telepathy, ensuring their conversation remained private. "The guns must be capable of shooting through the air, with everyone equipped to handle the firing velocity underwater. The impact must be significant enough to neutralize any distractions caused by someone being shot."

"We will proceed through the vent. You know its location, right?" the Millennial man asked.

"Yes, sir, I do," the old man replied. "The water is red near the vent, as the glacier water filters underground and is then released through the Silfra Fissure, which restores its pristine clarity. This removes the microscopic filaments that cause the water to turn red. These filaments primarily consist of actin polymers, interacting with various proteins in the cell. Microfilaments usually have a diameter of about 7 mm and are composed of two actin strands. As the water moves farther from the vent, it gradually lightens in color."

"You can gauge your proximity by the small fragmented waves of dark red in the water," the Millennial man added. "By passing through there, no human or machine can penetrate the water, only the Wobbaquas. The machinery you will build should have no trouble crossing into the other realm."

"Water-based materials are ideal as they can adapt and flow with the surroundings. You are the expert!" the Millennial man praised, smiling at the old man. "Once everything is finalized, you will receive fifty thousand shales, large golden coins. I want to see your family happy with what you have done for our underwater society. There will be no exceptions to the rules—you will become a wealthy Wobbaqua!" he proclaimed.

"There have been several aircraft crash-landings in the oceanic waters off the coast of Africa over the years," the Millennial man continued. "These could serve as a basis for constructing a magnificently large traveling cannon to target the culprits while submarines harvest the isopod beds. However, we must also consider the individuals from the submarines in smaller craft with diving gear. Once we capture and imprison them in our world, we must not forget the hidden ones with Tommy Hawk hatchets and Sharkskin holsters. They are the ones we need on our side," Millennial explained. "Those who do not align with our cause will be removed, and our world will be restored to harmony."

"We can disassemble the aircraft and bring them back for your crewmen to overhaul," the Millennial man suggested. Speaking authoritatively, the old man looked up. He said, "Between you and me, we can have a wide range of militia weapons ready to eliminate many within your timeframe."

"Yes, let us gather and commence the preparations tomorrow. My crews will be at the large World War II airplane hangar, and we can lay out the plans," the Millennial man proposed. "I will ensure they are categorized according to their expertise in their respective fields. Come, I will introduce you to them personally. We can use telepathy to communicate and coordinate the construction. It's similar to how computers work," the older man remarked. "We can zoom in on our meetings."

The Millennial man was surprised that the older Wobbaqua understood the extent of the project, including the required velocity of the weapons and the utilization of telepathic signals akin to computer data transmission. "The zoom feature is icing on the cake," he thought.

Months passed, and the hangars were filled with all the necessary materials while the crews diligently organized everything. The Millennial man monitored the progress daily through Zoom meetings with the old man. This continuous communication facilitated improvement in the situation.

When scavenging wrecked ships for supplies during the underwater war, it is important to be cautious of seagulls that may dive beneath the water to feed. It is crucial to understand their habits before entering the water where they are feeding small fish. Allow me to explain.

Seagulls are remarkably intelligent creatures. They can learn, remember, and even pass on behaviors. For instance, they have been observed stamping their feet in a group to imitate rainfall, tricking earthworms into coming to the surface. Their intelligence is further demonstrated through various feeding behaviors, such as dropping hard-shelled mollusks onto rocks to crack them open for consumption and following plows in fields where they know there will be an abundance of upturned grubs and other food sources.

Seagulls exhibit attentive and caring parental behavior. Males and females pair for life, taking turns incubating the eggs and providing food and protection to the chicks. They possess a complex and highly developed communication system consisting of various vocalizations and body movements.

One fascinating aspect of seagulls is their ability to drink fresh and saltwater, which is uncommon among animals and birds. They have specialized glands above their eyes that flush out salt from their systems through openings in their beaks.

There is considerable diversity among different gull species, with the smallest being the Little Gull (120 g and 29 cm) and the largest being the Great Black-beaked Gull (1.75 kg and 75 cm). They possess a small claw halfway up their lower leg, enabling them to sit and roost on high ledges without being blown off by strong winds.

Young gulls form nursery flocks where they play and learn essential skills for adulthood. While a few adult males often supervise these flocks, they remain together until the birds are old enough to breed.

In Native American symbolism, seagulls represent a carefree attitude, versatility, and freedom. Many seagulls have learned to conserve energy by hovering over bridges, absorbing rising heat from paved roadways. Brick Thunder said about salt lake City, seagulls are fondly remembered for assisting Mormon settlers with a cricket infestation. The seagull is now the state bird of Utah, and a monument in Salt Lake City commemorates the event known as the 'Miracle of the Gulls.'

The Graveyard

Before the war can commence, securing a proper resting place for those who may become immovable or deceased during the conflict is essential. These individuals will find peace in the sacred garden of the dead, where their soul spots will reside. Concrete pylons have been erected in the monumental graveyard next to the city, ensuring that the graves will remain above sea level and protected from intrusion by mammals. Each cement block resembles the entrance to a small tomb, creating a sacred space for loved ones to visit and grieve. As Millennial requested, decorations of seahorses and ginger adorn the front gate, and the walking aisles are meticulously manicured in vibrant green.

The monuments are crafted from the finest marble, with a few exceptional pieces made from white onyx. The smoothness and radiant shine of the onyx are almost blinding as the sun's rays seep through the openings, illuminating the statues of mermaid angels with their majestic outspread wings. These monuments serve as a testament to the families' love and devotion, representing the best they did for their loved ones while they were alive.

Certain unspoken matters are reserved for later discussions, allowing for a sense of calm and restraint. Many of the Wobbaquas have found healing from their afflictions, and the older members of the community come together in a solemn procession to assist in placing the departed in their final resting places. They offer prayers to the father, seeking his grace in healing the battle scars and injuries sustained during the siege. With long feathers, they sprinkle holy water on the sides of the graves, binding them with sharkskin and golden wire. Holding light canteens, they participate in the burial ceremony of a few elderly Wobbaquas on this day.

Keeping a distance from the holy water is advised, as its penetration into the skin may result in a unique and sacred transformation. Some might say it would resemble a porcupine without its quills, an otherworldly sight.

The number of humans involved in the war could be staggering. While we, the Wobbaquas, believe in providing a peaceful resting place for the soul spot when a Wobbaqua passes from this world to the next, it is unfortunate that humans often neglect such care for their counterparts.

Oil solidifiers and hydrocarbon-attracting polymers can be utilized when human remains become solidified. These substances, driven by Van der Waals forces, consist of porous matrices composed of long chains of hydrocarbons. They effectively bind to and encapsulate hydrocarbons such as oil and gasoline. However, when humans are left unattended, their bodies may be consumed by fish, often called watery graves. Larger fish, attracted by the scent, may feed on these remains as they wash ashore during the tides. It is crucial to have a plan to address these bodies' proper handling and disposal.

Millennial turned to John and asked if he could handle this matter. John readily agreed and stated, "Absolutely, Millennial! I will coordinate with the morgue in New York City to arrange for appropriate vessels and vehicles to transport the bodies to funeral homes or the morgue for proper handling."

John nodded in understanding. "I will ensure that each body is properly identified and records are maintained," he replied. "We will use their soul spot as a means of identification, and our telepathic abilities will assist in confirming their identity, including their place of residence and colony affiliation. I will oversee this process personally."

As for retrieving the bodies, John acknowledged the importance of handling them carefully. "We must be mindful of the delicate balance between the living and the deceased," he said. "We will coordinate with the authorities to ensure that the bodies are respectfully and safely removed from the grounds. Additionally, I will ensure that our shorelines are closely monitored to protect against any potential dangers, such as sharks approaching the shallows due to the effects of global warming."

The Millennial Man expressed appreciation and emphasized the significance of maintaining a harmonious coexistence with the living and the dead. With John's assurance, he felt confident that the necessary measures would be taken to address these important aspects of the war preparations.

The successful meeting filled the Millennial man with optimism and determination. The team had made significant progress in developing advanced weapons, including lasers, light waves, sliced water, and nitro. The armory was fully stocked and ready for battle, providing a range of options to combat the isopod threat.

As the mechanical weaponry moved back and forth through the area, being tested for accuracy and effectiveness, the hangars experienced some disturbance. However, these activities were necessary to ensure the weapons were in optimal condition for the upcoming battle.

The presence of sea-bed cars indicated the commitment to clearing the way for progress, even if it meant removing the bodies of the deceased. Cleaning up the aftermath of the war was a crucial step in restoring harmony to their underwater world.

The Millennial Man noticed the old Wobbaqua, standing nearby in worn-out overalls with a determined expression. The Millennial man understood the old man's commitment to the cause. He bid him farewell before diving into the deeper waters, disappearing into the abyss.

Filled with a renewed sense of purpose, Millennial prepared to face the challenges ahead, knowing that the combined efforts of the Wobbaqua warriors and their advanced weaponry would pave the way for a successful outcome in their battle against the isopod thieves.

As Millennial watched from beneath the surface, he noticed a new watercraft approaching. The old man had completed his preparations, ensuring that all the necessary equipment for battle was ready. He reminded everyone to be mindful of the spiders that inhabited these waters, particularly the seawater spiders.

Seawater spiders were a diverse species that dwelled in the ocean's depths. Their webs, which were deep purple, blue, and gray, crowded the waterways. Once the spiders finished feeding, these translucent webs were repurposed as nets. Although invisible to the naked eye, Wobbaquas had the unique ability to see them by turning sideways.

These spiders were quartered off toward the North American continent in the deep spaces between the Bermuda Triangle and Africa. Some possessed astonishing jumping abilities, capable of leaping across a pyramid. They fed on isopods when they could find them, with the mother spiders carrying their young on their backs. If a Wobbaqua fell prey to them, the spiders would swiftly consume the meat in seconds. The Millennial referred to them as acid spiders due to their formidable presence.

The Millennials saw the potential benefit of these spiders in the war against the cartel and their isopod mines. The seafloor teemed with spider eggs that hatched and rapidly grew into young spiders on their mother's back. The idea of these creatures entering the war arena sent chills down his spine. Still, he found humor in the fact that every habitat had its spider inhabitants, even if these happened to be gigantic.

Returning to his position in the mansion where the God was housed, Millennial prepared to meet with the Lord of the Underworld of the sea. To reach the meeting, he planned to navigate through the global ocean conveyor belt—a dynamic system of deep-ocean circulation driven by temperature and salinity. This constant movement of water plays a vital role in redistributing heat and nutrients around the globe.

As Millennial made his way, he couldn't help but notice the area lined with golden artifacts from shipwrecks, remnants of treasures left behind by sunken ships. These relics were a testament to the ocean's power and impact on human history. The echoes of hurricane activity served as a reminder of the ever-changing and powerful nature of the sea.

Millennial embraced his role as a water lord, growing into a fine specimen of leadership as he faced the challenges and responsibilities ahead.

The Wobbaquas, adorned in intricately designed armory-type clothing, wore fine linen as a loincloth and a breastplate of gold inscribed with the story of their origins when they first arrived from space and settled along the seaside, marking the beginnings of the Wobbaqua civilization. Their helmets accentuated their faces, making them appear awe-inspiringly beautiful to any being in the universe. As sea warriors and rulers of the underwater world, they stood above all others.

The gatekeeper could raise portions of the smaller parts of the city to the oceanic surface. Raising these parts at different intervals eliminates mold or sedimentation from the sea through exposure to sunlight. These raised portions were only exposed if the sun was high, ensuring their preservation.

Before the equinox of the moon rising nightly, each part would be returned to its place. Wobbaquas were trained to manage their trade, while the outer structure could only touch the shell casings.

During maintenance, many pieces of sea glass were removed and reset. It was a delicate process that required precision. Often, the babies of the Wobbaquas were brought to the surface as a learning drill, taken from the sacks of jellyfish. This exposed them to the knowledge that there was another world above the waters they called home, much like how humans look up and believe in the existence of a place called Heaven.

The presence of seashores and migrating pelicans added a unique touch to the lives of the Wobbaquas. The mating habits of the pelicans differed from those of the deep-sea creatures. American white pelicans, in particular, were serially monogamous birds that formed pairs for one breeding season. They engaged in courtship rituals, displaying their bright orange bills, strutting, bowing, and taking short flights to attract a mate. Once they found a partner, they engaged in a romantic dance together. These pelicans annually migrated, with some resident populations in the Gulf of Mexico and Mexico. Juveniles started their first migration to the winter range in their second year of life.

During migration, the pelicans flew in large flocks, often consisting of more than 180 individuals. They exhibited graceful flight, spreading their wings and sliding onto the water's surface with their feet. They typically flew in linear formations or V shapes, gliding and flapping their wings. On days with favorable updrafts, they could soar.

Although they did not dive, they were strong swimmers with subcutaneous air sacs in their breasts that provided buoyancy. Being gregarious birds, they were always found in groups while roosting, nesting, or foraging. Nesting colonies were large and densely populated, often hosting around 1,000 nests. These natural elements and wildlife added to the vibrant tapestry of the underwater world and the lives of the Wobbaquas.

Millennial, aware of the importance of their role as a leader in the upcoming war, emphasizes the need for cleanliness and dignity in their presence as they gather for the meeting. He acknowledges that his brother serves as the temple's keeper, symbolizing their society's highest level of purity and holiness.

With plans in order, the focus of the meeting will be on strategizing how to wage war against the upper world. Millennial understands the gravity of the situation and the importance of his role as a leader. He must exhibit diligence and exceptional leadership skills to guide his people effectively.

Comparing himself to a meticulous writer using a quill, Millennial emphasizes the importance of clear and direct communication. Instructions and directions must be delivered legibly, leaving no room for confusion or misinterpretation.

Millennial's commitment to upholding manners, couth, and effective communication reflects his dedication to leading his people with integrity and ensuring the success of their mission.

Chapter Nine
The Temple

Once immersed in the beauty of the sea, he reminisced about the landmarks etched in his mind over a lifetime spent in its depths. The Millennial Man swam towards the entrance of the Wobbaqua world, marveling at the ruins that cleverly concealed it. These ruins held a majestic civilization, proud and grand. The pyramids had inspired their design found adorning their sea-shore, the only structure they knew while growing up beside the ancient remnants.

Approaching the gate, he tried pulling the massive handle, as he always did, but it remained immovable. Remembering the words of his counterpart, Orbital Man, about a forthcoming battle, he stood there puzzled. "You will know what it will take to open the gate when one arrives," Orbital man had said.

Then, as if by magic, he recalled the shining flying woman hood ornament, which was often removed from the war wagon's hood in the past. He placed it onto the handle, and to his amazement, the woman's wings unfolded, emitting a radiant light from her head. Siren sounds filled the air, and water bubbles appeared as the gate creaked open, releasing the Wobbaqua warriors into the sea world. It was a bittersweet moment, as he couldn't help but think of the lives lost needlessly due to a battle that should have never happened.

Swimming through the vibrant coral-colored area and pristine aqua-colored water, he felt invigorated. His fins released a flow of aqua-colored water, and he luxuriated in its warmth against his skin, playfully swimming, turning cartwheels, and maneuvering through the inviting waters. He admired the massive golden walls that lined the city entrance, leading to its beautiful passageways. Finally, at peace with himself and his majestic world, he felt a sense of pride.

Carvings from the Egyptian days still prevail, forming a massive gate that captivates him with its intricate and breathtaking details. Each carving serves as a memory lane, revealing the history and existence of this world. Slowly peeling back the layers of memories, he reflects on his mistakes and accomplishments. With a telepathic gesture, he slides the gate open and closed effortlessly. At the same time, Orbital Man observes, and his soul brother fixes the gate's apparatus. The gate operates with solar energy, controlled by his mind.

Two majestic Wobbaquas are carved on each side of the golden-laced gate. Above them, a gigantic figure akin to Mount Rushmore depicts the faces of the unseen voice from centuries past. Wing walls flank the walkway street in the depths, and a massive warning bell hangs beside the entrance. If danger threatens the city, the bell will ring and alert all good-hearted Wobbaquas magically.

The street tiles are carved to represent significant Wobbaquas who have impacted their aquatic world. These carvings, inscribed with a hint of moss green, symbolize the connection between the underwater Wobbaquas and the land. Adjacent to the roadway, many bodies hang, waiting for their families to claim them. Anyone who dares to destroy these sacred carvings will face severe consequences without question. It is a simple but effective law to deter naughty behavior.

As the massive gate opens, he gazes upon the perfect world he has cherished for so long. However, he can't help but worry about it becoming a nightmare if he doesn't have a direct and steadfast battle plan before the war against drugs begins.

He sends a sea falcon, a bird of pristine blue, with a vital message to Inspector Thunder, who resides in the upper world's metroplex. The falcon arrives at Thunder's window, delivering the scroll that outlines the battle plan. Thunder is amazed by the majestic bird's size and wonders about the scale of what they are dealing with.

Upon opening the scroll, Thunder discovers a small cylinder designed exclusively for his purpose. As he places it into his computer's hard drive, a watery world unfolds before him—the city of the Wobbaquas, a place he could never have imagined. Intrigued and wide-eyed, he contemplates the future of humankind on the planet.

"They must clean this up," he thought, deeply concerned as he witnessed the massive isopod fields and the drug cartel's submarines causing extensive destruction to the underwater world. He felt the urgency to stop this in both the human and Wobbaqua worlds. A telepathic voice reached Thunder, emphasizing the need to join forces to protect their shared world from distress.

Thunder, in awe, agreed to meet the speaker at the docks to further discuss their plan at sea, near the largest boulder off the coastline and over the Mariana Trench. The meeting would be secretive, with Thunder providing the coordinates for the location.

He knew he had trusted allies who could help find this hidden spot.

As he finished watching the video, Thunder contemplated the gravity of the situation, causing goosebumps on his arms. He stored the date and time of the meeting securely in his memory banks to keep it confidential. Taking the disk to save the video, he felt an inexplicable heat in his hand. To his surprise, the disk transformed into translucent water, slipping through his fingers and leaving no trace of the underwater world records.

Realizing that he was communicating with a fish-man, a Millennial man, Thunder acknowledged the possibility of a civilization of fish-like people who could transform into human form. This revelation made him consider the unpredictable nature of future events.

The increasing pollution on seashores had drawn the attention of the Wobbaquas, prompting them to surface and take part in cleaning up the beaches and shorelines. Millennial noticed this as he emerged from the depths to meet with Brick Thunder, emphasizing the urgency of their mission.

The story takes a fascinating turn, blending elements of mystery, magic, and environmental awareness. Thunder and Millennial man's collaboration holds the promise of an extraordinary adventure with both worlds at stake.

Return of the Falcon

With wings spread and a majestic sea-blue hue, the sea falcon stands grandly before the father. With a nod, the sea falcon is sent back to Thunder, carrying the message of the meeting place and other important details. Its destiny is to be a carrier falcon, serving the upper class of the Wobbaqua world in secrecy.

Millennial recalls the massive dungeon where thousands of sea falcons fly into cages of a specific size. They are their breed, essential for all colonies, and kept beneath the father's house. The pyramids, with numerous caverns beneath them, serve various purposes. Millennial embraces open-minded thinking and remembers his brother standing at the father's resting place inside the massive temple within the pyramid. The prophecies and instructions given by the father are etched in his memory, guiding their enormous undertaking to create a hiding place in the ocean where Wobbaquas can live both on land and in the sea.

Safety is found in the temple, housing the Father's spirit to guide the Wobbaquas. Only Millennial and Orbital Man can see the father's vault. They are beings from another world, directed to conduct civilization to goodness and housed where they can exist even if others have disintegrated into the seawater. A tall podium with a shining light at the top serves as the father-speaking place, where their hearts are known as soon as they enter it.

The voice from the other side, existing since the temple's construction, speaks wisdom to them. The Rosetta stone, a subject of curiosity for all inhabitants of Earth, is mentioned by Orbital.

Time seems to stand still for Millennial and Orbit man as they navigate the waters of longevity, aware of their place in the millennium and the possibility of transformation.

Returning to his home in the city, Millennial contemplates tomorrow, especially the challenge of the stuck gate handle. He knows he must prepare and present his battle plan to military generals and plan seekers. The warehouses are filled with metal seahorses and "four-wheelers" to protect the oceanic civilization. A podcast is created to inform everyone before the battlefield is set, ensuring the success of their life-saving mission and battle plan.

Warrior Women

These vehicles are all powered by solar energy and trans-fusion, derived from a block of radiation beneath the magnificently large battlefield surface. Many shelled protrusions come to the forefront to be carried on the backs of the warrior women who will join their male counterparts in the deep. Many Wobbaquas have adopted dressing habits of both genders, customizing their appearance with eye-fixing and choices like lip color or ties. Wild Wobbaquas who have come to fight are hazed, with some serving as foot enslaved people to the Wobbaqua team, their scales missing, leaving them somewhat naked.

Their weapons include bows and arrows, holstered neatly in shark skin pouches for easy handling, with straps made of strewn shells. The pouches have a unique grip, smooth in one direction and strong in the other due to nicks on the scales, a reminder of past battles. The arrows are crafted from straightened fossilized sea worms, filed to sharp tips. At the same time, the bows are made from waves of petrified fins painted to resemble Wobbaqua flesh.

Jet ski-type vehicles with rotors on the sides await them, capable of covering long distances underwater at high speeds. These crafts are fashioned from old bent submarine shells, welded together to create space-age four-wheeler jet skis. Equipped with the ability to shoot water four stories high, they can easily hinder opponents. The back of these vehicles carries four spears loaded with Nitro, serving as additional weapons. On the sides, guns are designed to throw shell casings back into the backend for reloading.

Beneath the shell of the vehicles, cannons are held with a ball and a short twig that ignites when pulled, propelling projectiles up to three hundred feet into the depths or onto the shore, wherever the battle takes place. Some old war wagons, worn down by saltwater erosion, sit alongside the battlefield, contrasting with today's pristine and water-worthy weaponry.

Amidst the preparation for war, horses with metal silver and gray headgear await, equipped to keep them breathing. As the real modern-day war wagon appears, it becomes challenging to identify the occupants until they recognize none other than...

The highlight of the battle is the War Wagon of Pacific Blue, a 1938 model Ford transformed into a lowered and souped-up four-door coupe equipped with a gunner on top. The doors flip open, revealing a tabletop with a firing station for the gunners to harness themselves. These gunners are trained to operate a weapon that shoots blasts of radioactive materials into the water, limiting the movement of the Wobbaquas in that area. The turtle hull at the back houses a shot of pulsating force generated from lignite coal residue, delivering a powerful shock to anything behind the wagon.

The tire covers open, releasing blasts of dynamite aimed from the sides, and the headlights, covered in sea glass, flip into halogen lighting, blinding anything that sees it. The underbearing frame, raised by hydraulics, contains various projectiles that release red-colored water, poisoning the air bubbles and affecting anything within the battlefield's confines.

One crucial element of the War Wagon is colored water at the end of the battle. It clears out the dead and injured Wobbaquas and disinfects the seawater where the bodies lie for too long.

The operation of this wagon requires well-trained warriors, and those who don't follow instructions will face deadly consequences. The Ol' man emphasizes that understanding and skill are vital, and those who fail to grasp it will perish.

Chapter Ten

Ol' FisherMan: The Battle

Radiation becomes a factor as it is sprayed into the water, shocking anything within a five-hundred-foot radius. The War Wagon demonstrates its power, with missiles guided by a driver inside. To the amazement of onlookers, the driver turns out to be none other than the Ol' man, sitting on a syrup bucket with his legs barely reaching the pedals.

Millennial man and Orbital man watch the impressive demonstrations, realizing that they must take action against the drug cartel, which has trapped many teenagers into slave labor. The old black war wagon plunges into the oceanic water, causing a huge blast of bubbles and demonstrating the need for additional measures to free the Wobbaquas from the cartel's grasp.

They plan to press the culprits into the oceanic waters, utilizing the pressure chamber where the invisible beings dwell. These creatures move slowly and suffocate anything in their path, making it dangerous to traverse. They require extra-fine weaponry and magical assistance from the father to tackle this challenge.

The Millennial man knows the location of a great aircraft graveyard and old shipwreck, offering a source of metal for crafting weapons. His skilled craft workers are ready to implement his suggestions and expertise in weapon development.

The Millennial Man removes the chrome shining flying lady hood ornament from the War Wagon, keeping it in his pocket, and others dare not question his actions, respecting his eminent power.

The narrative unveils an exciting plan to equip the Wobbaquas with the necessary arsenal to confront their adversaries and rescue their fellow Wobbaquas from enslavement. The future remains uncertain, but Millennial man's determination and preparedness hold the promise of a fierce and compelling battle for justice.

The Deep

Emerging from the depths, a magnificent army of thousands of tall Wobbaquas rises to the occasion, fully dressed in warrior attire and equipped with bronze breastplates and Chinese woven silk sackcloth. They march precisely and form a military formation, guided by instructions from the Millennial and Orbital men, who have planned the upcoming battle in a secret cave beneath the pyramids.

The Wobbaquas have assembled an impressive array of weaponry, including vehicles, submarines, and ground-to-air crafts. Many are skilled with fire-blowing dragons, ready to unleash their power during the fierce undertaking. Above the water, millions of seabirds are circling in preparation for the battle. The atmosphere is charged with energy and determination as the warriors wait for their destination and instructions.

Each Wobbaqua wears a headdress helmet with fish skin strings, which catch the light from aquatic lightning bugs, illuminating the vast underwater army. They are dressed in uniform formation, displaying a rainbow of colors that signify their ranks and branches of service. Their weapons, ammunition, and armor are crafted carefully and ingeniously.

The warriors are prepared with various weaponry, including nitro-filled ammo and grenades crafted from molten lava and electricity. The ammunition is designed to cause powerful explosions on contact, making them formidable opponents.

The clothing and equipment are engineered to allow easy movement through waterways and use air ducts under the city for stealth attacks. Gray aircraft material from Venice is used for maneuverability, combining lightweight properties and buoyancy in the water.

The Millennials and Orbital Man salute the brave Wobbaquas, ready to defend their underwater world. With their arms raised in a salute and pride shining in their eyes, they admire the courage and dedication of these warriors. Sitting on his water scooter, the Ol' man waits at the rear of the procession, ready to enter the pyramid and await the call to arms.

As the tension mounts and preparations are made, the Wobbaquas stand ready for the impending battle against the drug cartel and the fight to protect their cherished underwater civilization.

The Orbital man communicates with the father about the plan, ensuring that both worlds understand the consequences of their actions and the need for cooperation. Meanwhile, Millennial Man explains his recent shivers caused by being in a dry environment for too long. He will rehydrate and wait for his body to absorb oxygen from seawater to recover.

With preparations in place and details sorted out, Millennial and Orbital stand before a gigantic computer screen, mentally sharing information to devise a plan based on the father's guidance. The father's voice echoes through the temple, leaving a blue hue on the walls as he communicates telepathically with the two.

The father approves of their justification and provides insight into the upcoming war. He shares a surprise strategy to destroy the adversaries and restructure the isopod beds for the Wobbaquas' benefit. Millennial takes out a blue sea glass, a symbol of the frozen military of another civilization, ready to assist when needed.

The frozen warriors wait in a state of suspended animation, freezing themselves in mid-water until the time comes for them to spring into action. When the war begins, they are prepared to follow Millennials' and their commander's commands.

With the plan in place and the support of the father and the frozen warriors, Millennial and Orbital are ready to face the impending battle, determined to protect their underwater world and end the threat posed by the drug cartel.

Chapter Eleven
War Beside the City

Assembled for war, the hovercraft and all its weapons have been prepared for the war-driven area of the sea. Many are ready to come ashore if necessary to liberate the drug traders from the bondage of the drug lords. They walk in and out of different stores, trying to find the kingpin drug dealer, but to no avail. Eventually, they return to the streets.

As they come down the street, they pick up everyone in the group of undercover officers. The lead officers are driving, with Harold, one of the older ones on the force, usually scoffing at the rest for safety reasons. Harold is a bit of a loner, but he knows the street life in New York City.

They stop in front of the group, and while the vehicle is still rolling, they open the two doors of the fifty-five Chevy, which comes to a screeching stop. Each one jumps into the vehicle and takes a seat. Brick jumps in the backseat and feels cramped. Looking around, he spots his buddy Grady with Butch waxed hair walking down the sidewalk, looking surprised to see this group together. Grady sees the driver's side seat flipped up, and Harold motions for him to come on.

Grady jumps into the back seat, squeezing his way behind the driver. The motor rumbles loudly, and the exhaust pipe is loose, making plenty of noise. Making eye contact with the two already in the back seat, Thunder speaks up.

"Hi, Grady!" Thunder greeted. "I heard you were sick, seeing it multiple times on social media, in and out of the hospital."

Thunder turned to look at Grady from top to bottom and noticed how skinny and unhealthy he appeared. "Proud to see you here, though, under the circumstances," Thunder remarked. "We need all the help we can get!"

"We have to stop these punks," Grady said angrily, pointing out, "Thunder, they are killing three times more young people than your force ever anticipated." His face showed his age, marked with wrinkles, and he looked dirty as if he had been on the streets for a long time. "Damn, dude, hurry over! I'm cramped as hell in here!" Thunder complained, trying to stretch his long legs.

Reluctantly, Grady scooted over across the long backseat to make room for Thunder. As he looked around, he saw that Harold was the driver. Harold's sideburns were extra-long, with gray streaks mingling in his black hair, and he appeared to be a seasoned undercover police officer.

"If it gets too crowded, just roll down the windows and let the air take your mind off the situation," Harold suggested as he whipped the steering wheel side to side, navigating through the residential apartment sky-rise areas of New York City.

"Dude, where did you get your driver's license?" Thunder exclaimed, holding onto a strap hanging from the car's headliner. The man riding in the passenger seat turned and smiled, an older man with wrinkles and missing a few teeth, yet experienced in his purpose. Thunder looked surprised, gape-mouthed, and shook his head. Then, he refocused on the situation, his forehead wrinkled with worry, making him look like a bulldog.

"Man, straighten that face! We'll be okay!" Grady yelled across the parking lot as they hurriedly left the area.

"Shut the hell up! We have to get out of here as fast as we can!" Thunder responded, his voice tense with urgency. "This area is so bad; they'll strip the car with us. They'll gut us, throw our bodies in the trunk, and drive around all day!"

Harold whipped the steering wheel, trying to dodge the rain of bullets from machine guns, making the car swerve from side to side. They saw people running for cover as they desperately tried to roll faster. "Let's roll! Let's roll!" Thunder urged from the window.

Suddenly, a man appeared behind the car, wielding an ooze and shooting at them. "Watch out!" Grady warned. "This guy's a true driver!" The man skillfully whipped around the corner, losing a hubcap, which shot away from the wheel and slapped against the storefront of the Express Bail Bond office adjacent to the judicial complex.

As they continued driving, they encountered a roadblock of orange cones manned by drug cartel members, preventing traffic from reaching the Hudson Bay area. Thunder, holding onto the strap, realized how this obstacle could play in their favor to accomplish their mission.

The reality of the situation hit Thunder hard as he realized that insiders were working against them. These traitors were dressed as street workers, making it essential for Thunder to cover his face, not wanting to be recognized by influential figures who might be involved.

"Damn, of all days, I must wear a yellow shirt!" Harold lamented, worried about being easily identifiable to those in high places who had shown up on the streets that day.

"Get ready, boys. We might have to fight out of this," Thunder said, stomping on the accelerator. Harold gripped the steering wheel tightly as the Chevy spewed smoke and gas fumes from its exhaust pipes, obscuring their view from the gunman behind them. A bullet hit the back window, shattering it, and glass fragments flew everywhere.

"Are you hit?" Thunder asked, concerned about his companions' safety.

"No, hell no! Just get us out of here!" Grady exclaimed.

They sped towards the harbor, where a boat was waiting to take them to the location of the weekly isopod dust pickup. Leaning back in the backseat, Thunder saw the water ahead and felt relief. "There! We've outrun the bullets, people!" Harold announced.

"Stop being so sarcastic, Harold," Thunder retorted, still on edge from their intense situation.

Meanwhile, Thunder climbed out of the backseat of the two-door Chevy, rushing behind Grady as they sought cover from the shooting. They quickly made their way onto a waiting boat, throwing the rope onto the deck and preparing to take off. Grady embraced Thunder, expressing his gratitude for Thunder's service to the people of New York. Looking back, they saw Harold speed away in the lowrider yellow Chevy, disappearing. Thunder smiled, feeling the camaraderie among them.

"Thanks, Grady," Thunder replied, touched by the appreciation. "That means a lot to me!" He then pointed towards a street crossing and mentioned his lady friend, Thalia Hunter, who lived in an apartment building nearby.

With a determined and confident demeanor, thunder decided to go back to see her.

The other men parked the vehicle and started cranking the boat's engine. After a short while, Thunder returned from the edge of the building. They all held on as they headed to sea to catch up with the freighter. Preparing for the upcoming encounter, they gathered ammunition, vests, grenades, and assault rifles, anticipating what they would face on the freighter.

Thunder removed his yellow shirt and hid it in the boat's toolbox, replacing it with a camouflage shirt. He made a mental note not to wear the yellow shirt again. As they approached the Hudson Bay area, they knew that law enforcement deputies were waiting for a leader to bring about the capture of the drug cartel workers assembling there to collect the manufactured isopod dust.

"Once we reach the top deck of the freighter, right before dark," Thunder explained, returning to the group with a green shirt, making him hardly recognizable among them.

"Men, we are here to end the destruction of our children's lives!" Thunder exclaimed passionately. "We must make this happen; stop those burning our city from the inside out, ruining countless lives. It's up to us to take a stand!"

"We know the risks, but this is what we live for, right? " Thunder continued, rallying the group.

"Right!" The men responded in unison, raising their hands and cheering loudly.

"Hell, yes! Let's get them!" Thunder declared, the determination in his voice evident.

The boat's motor hummed softly as they approached where the divers were expected to emerge. Many men were dressed in scuba gear, ready to slide into the dark water beside the boat.

"They are professional divers, well-versed in the area," Thunder explained. "They've been waiting for the right moment to capture these culprits who surface with the manufactured dust."

As they continued their mission, the night at sea was calm and serene, with moonlight illuminating the smooth oceanic waters around them. The team was focused and determined to end the drug cartel's operations and protect their community.

"Professionals know what they're doing," Thunder reaffirmed. Their expertise allowed them to snare another diver with a hook before they knew what was happening. As soon as the boat came to a stop, an immense bale of bundled strings resembling black burlap emerged from the depths of the sea. The boat experienced a surge, but the team remained silent and focused, trying to raise the bundle to the awaiting freighter's height.

Then, one of Thunder's men, a skilled diver, shot a blasting cap from an arrow, hitting a strap holding the illegal goods. The explosion lit up the vessel's side, causing them to release the dust back into the sea, which affected those without scuba gear, drowning some. The sunrise found them wrapping up the operation and shutting it down. They spotted a shark approaching but were relieved when a fellow diver, Millennial, emerged from the depths and protected the humans from the shark's threat. They were far from shore, and the tide carried the bundles into the bay area.

Thunder radioed ahead to have the bundles harvested from the oceanic waters and taken in for disposal to save the world from this dangerous drug. This massive drug bust was replicated on each continent, making it one of the largest ever encountered. However, things took a dangerous turn when a water plane arrived to gather the excess boxes from the water, and a shot was fired, causing the plane to burst into flames and crash into the bay. The pilot tragically burned to death before impact.

Thunder noted the plane's number with a searchlight and sent it to investigators for further action. This led to the arrest of individuals connected to the drug bust. Thunder commented, "This has turned into a rich man's game, it seems," suggesting that powerful forces might be involved in the drug cartel's operations. The team knew that they were up against formidable adversaries. Still, they remained committed to eradicating the drug trade and protecting their community.

A solemn stillness enveloped the scene, something so eerie that it seemed beyond belief. Thunder felt a chill of fear inside him, realizing that this calm water would soon become a bloodbath. He silently prayed for everyone involved, knowing the dangerous nature of their mission.

Ling-too boats, operated by people of Asian nationality, were scattered in the distance, keeping an eye out for trouble since they knew the drug harvest was underway. These boats drifted slowly, their occupants carrying machine guns and a small light hanging from the side of their vessels. Thunder recognized them and gave instructions to his team, well aware of their intentions.

"If they jeopardize our mission to stop this mess," Thunder stated firmly, "shoot them and sink their boats. We know they are out here looking to steal and sell bundles themselves."

Disappointment laced as he added, "Our Asian buddies and the rag heads are all part of this. The city is full of them. They would do anything for the money they make from this harvest, even betray their own."

Thunder sighed and quietly muttered, "Greed turns people into useless individuals. That's just my opinion."

As they closed in on their target, Thunder reflected on the battle they were fighting, comparing it to an epidemic originating from China and spreading worldwide. He criticized the city's hasty reopening decision, which led to another epidemic. The drug trade and its consequences were like a disease infecting society. Thunder was determined to stop it at all costs.

Chapter Twelve

The War in the Abyss

"The virus spread and happened, and many have died. Maybe people will learn from previous mistakes and be able to bring forth knowledge to outrun situations." Thunder continues.

Spinner turned to look at Thunder with an exclamatory expression of disgust. "Thunder, you know what all this is about, don't you?" he said.

"Yessirree, I sure do." Thunder said. "When things are strolled about, we have to gather them back the way we want them, my O.C. Disorder says."

"Should we have to, we will go to the Continental Divide to decipher how the underwater currents flow. That could be used in the upper world. Deciding which way the rivers and streams flow could be helpful to some, so keep that in mind. It doesn't matter as long as your quiver is full." He said.

Beneath the oceanic waters, the Wobbaquas are uniting to form an army, determined to fight for what rightfully belongs to them—the right to life for all Wobbaquas. This struggle may be connected to the isopod distribution. The situation becomes more complex as the water wagon freezes miles of designated seawater, effectively blocking the drug cartel's access to the area. The cartel is keen on obtaining the valuable isopod dust.

The machine distributes the ice once the seawater is frozen, creating a temporary barrier. However, it will eventually have to return to the area and thaw out the seawater so that those who need to come and go can pass freely through the water again.

Thunder possesses knowledge of where the water is currently frozen. With the help of the Millennials, they may lead a freighter to that specific area. This strategic move allows the Wobbaquas to gather the isopod dust directly from the ship, effectively preventing the cartel from removing it.

By securing the isopod dust and ensuring it remains on the ship's deck, the Wobbaquas aim to safeguard their rights and protect their underwater domain from outside interference. The battle for control over these resources continues, with Thunder and the Wobbaquas facing formidable challenges in their quest to preserve their way of life.

The millennial man exclaimed while watching the freighter coming from a distance, "This battle could go on for years! It has been a long road. A Wobbaqua possesses a remarkable ability to stand at the edge of seawater, rendering themselves invisible to the naked eye. They have mastered the art of transforming into an iridescent and hollow form, akin to the elusive ghosts of the seawater—appearing and disappearing swiftly."

Emerging from a distance are the water suckers, known as water angels. Explaining it further, Thunder mentions, "These creatures have a distinctive structure with green wings that extend over vast areas. They function like sponges, absorbing pollutants from the seawater. Massive creatures!"

As they approach, they seem to be flying, diluted by seawater, and they consume the water while excreting freshwater. Their secretions possess a unique property that dissolves any foreign particles in the seawater, effectively removing impurities and contaminants. Thunder believes that Millennials might have summoned these creatures, as their presence prevents sharks and predator fish from approaching, allowing a safe environment for clean-up.

In the aquatic world, a saying is similar to the human phrase, "Don't let me die with my boots on." They express the desire not to be eaten by fish when they reach their final moments, emphasizing the eternity of life in the depths.

Thunder playfully exchanges banter with someone named Harold, telling him to be quiet and receiving a smile in response.

After finishing their investigation, Thunder and the investigators return to the shore to rest. Thunder leaves the docking area and makes his way to a small apartment, enjoying the company of a lovely lady he knows, who welcomes him with an open-door concept.

Knowing that tomorrow will bring more challenges, Thunder seeks the rest and relaxation he needs tonight. As the night unfolds, he disappears into the darkness, and playful activities can be heard from within the apartment. It appears that Thunder enjoys rough play and humor in his private time.

The War

The battle beneath the ocean rages on, with long-statured fish and other creatures joining the war effort. They slither through the kelp beds, organizing weapons and clearing the aftermath of explosions. The fallen bodies are gathered by land-crawling fish and taken to a steaming branch of an erupting oceanic volcano, where they disintegrate.

The wise man acknowledges the grim reality of the war, knowing that those who signed up to defend the underwater world knew the risks. Their families will be cared for in return for their sacrifice, akin to an insurance policy. Once the sea beds are clean, the seabed crawling fish return to their place in the kelp beds, ready to assist if needed.

Millennial men are crucial in preparing the battleground, strategically placing equipment, and summoning various creatures like war hounds and black sea cats to guard the weapons. They know the majestic structures and inhabitants below the battlegrounds, awaiting the moment to rise and engage in battle.

The battle plans are set, and Millennial, having been summoned from the North Pole, coordinates the efforts to defend the underwater city and drive humans back to dry land. He receives vital information through telepathy, using a small piece of sea glass with a star map reflecting coordinates and instructions. The warriors are given the same information through their thought banks, and each group, including the Indians with their seahorses and bows and arrows, is assigned specific entry points into the battlefield.

As the war continues, the underwater world faces drastic measures to defend itself, with Millennial and his allies leading the charge to protect their community from destruction.

"Then, Frozen from the North, they can stop at the Indian Ocean while waiting for the battle to start. There, they have trillions of Dumbo octopuses they can eat to keep their strength while in that area. I will summon them when the time is at hand," Millennial said, strategizing precisely.

As the battle unfolds, the Bucklebacks come into action, a formidable war machine. With legs raised and holding weapons designed to blow water at incredible speeds, they are a force to be reckoned with. They await the command to engage on the other side of the prehistoric animal bone beds. Millennial feels concerned over the loss of the turnip beds and the potential impact on the perfect Wobbaqua Aquaculture.

The war begins, and the barrel-chested Bucklebacks, decked in leather-strapped gear, emerge from afar. Nearly a thousand troops group, awaiting Millennial's signal to proceed. Some of the Bucklebacks seem unfamiliar with the barge of foliage in the depths and inadvertently trample down the turnip patch beds, disrupting the plan.

Millennial warriors, led by Ol man, come in from the south with personally designed tanks and fast weapon-busted vehicles. They aim to close in and thwart the mafia's plans, destroying their mines and dismantling their structures.

Whales have gathered in the middle of the ocean around the city, providing a defensive barrier against anything that might hinder the removal of the culprits from the underwater world.

Millennial emphasizes removing the Wobbaquas from the mines before using ammunition to blow them up. The human drug cartel, the enemy they face, will not remain passive during this assault.

Despite the challenges, they have progressed, taking out smaller mines and infiltrating the enemy's ranks. Now, they face the daunting task of tackling the largest mine, requiring all their resources and equipment to succeed.

The battle is far from over, and the stakes are high. Millennial and his allies are prepared to face the dangers that lie ahead to protect their underwater world.

The head Buckleback holds a meeting with Millennials to discuss the future role of the Bucklebacks. They plan to clean up the battlefield, eliminating hostile threats swiftly and non-lethally. The Bucklebacks will shoot to incapacitate, like smashing a finger rather than cutting it off to send a clear message to potential troublemakers.

Millennial acknowledges the power of word of mouth among the Wobbaquas, knowing that news of their formidable presence will spread, serving as a deterrent for future disturbances. The Bucklebacks take pride in being an exceptional breed, nurtured by Jellyfish to become skilled and honorable warriors.

Millennial reminds them of the reason for the war and their purpose in fighting—to restore the honor of the Wobbaquas and the underwater world. With a resounding stomp of their fins, Millennial emphasizes their role as proud warriors, determined to protect their realm and bring about positive change.

The Bucklebacks stand united in their commitment, ready to fulfill their duty as fierce defenders of the underwater world and to restore peace and harmony to their homes.

Open Carry

All Wobbaquas are directed to carry weapons precisely when outside the domes. Protecting one another is the law of the underwater world since so many are carnivorous and will eat any flesh, only for the waterborne ones.

Seems that when the isopods are removed from the depths of the hot oceanic waters of the deep. This changes the structure and chemical balance of the seawater. The structure is even off-balance. Such a change in the seawater causes plankton and kelp beds to die.

"The oxygenation of the water is removed, and feeder fish die, so the larger fish do not come to feed. This leaves them to feed off the Wobbaqua kelp beds. That is too close to the domes for comfort." Millennial said.

Looking up, there are small farm bubble vehicles. Field workers drive each to rekindle the kelp beds back to perfection.

"Having said this, we must remedy all these changes to control the echo system in our world. The culprit fish and such come from the depths of the abyss to feed. Nothing can come in the way of our system of controlling the seaworthy environment. Things don't change the ratio of survival of the many life forms. Those that make up the underwater world of the Wobbaquas." Millennial said.

"The Wobbaquas must carry weapons to survive the travel from one colony to the other. This leaves too many dead feeders fish. The beaches are covered with stench. Dead fish, maggot, and fly infestation. Where there were once white, clean sandy beaches, with the structure in hand, the Wobbaquas will finish the battle and return everything to normal. With the help of the

Bucklebacks. Standard works for the Wobbaqua government. A loyal Wobbaqua, he replenished all the upper kelp beds. Returning the beaches to sandy white and the stench of dead rotting fish covered by the flocks of feeding seabirds.

Sure, it is a blessing for the birds to come. They will keep the seashores clean. Dive into the water for the feeding of floating dead objects. "Besides what the Bucklebacks have taken to the depths to do away with. Each who uses the open carry rule must be registered to carry. Should a fatality happen, they will be accepted. None rejected through the judicial system we have implemented." Millennial said.

"Then our judging individuals is different. Because we read the soul spot, a lie cannot live there without being detected." Orbital said.

The women pioneers of the underworld come as a battalion to protect the shale beds. Where they house the surroundings of the baby Wobbaqua nursery, these troopers are eye-full, their skin looking like a pair of bell-bottom pants and their upper body covered with ammo belts. It lays upon their skin, exposing a breast now and then like the mermaids.

"They have long fins that flow in the seawater. They have A.K. forty-sevens dangling beside their legs. They have on a sharkskin belt to hold all the handguns they carry. Finding one of these unarmed would be a disaster. Each one is an armed aquifer!" Millennial said.

The finest marksmen train these sea women. Each is blatantly trained for anything the depths have to offer. They are colonized to accomplish what they intended to guard. Mounted with swords. The finest shining-bladed Asian swords.

Seawomen wear the equipment designed for each. With a sword mounted on the leg side. A blade in the housing of the helmet and a dagger at the breastplate. A ninja sword mounted across the backs.

Awaiting at the outside of the domes. They hide inside a bubble of air to be unseen by any predators. Those that may come into the vicinity of the underwater world. Millennials license them to travel as far as they deem necessary. Protecting the world they live in. Telecommunication is a must since there are so many. They channel their thoughts to recognize all things in the world they are destined to protect. Many are born into their position and started as warriors early on.

"But these Millennials are so sexy looking," Marlina said while looking out the portal into the depths.

"That is a living here; we do not look at them that way. To us, they are a form of protection for the colonies." Millennial said.
"

"My world must be a safe place for us all. That was broken with the onset of the Isopods being harvested, and too many are finding our world. It may take a hundred years to get our privacy back. Marrying my Marlina may open yet another door to our society becoming one world." Millennial said.

"Remember, my love. There will never be a doubt that will be bestowed upon you. Not one while you are in my world. Conversely, you will be more in danger in the upper world than in the underworld." Millennial said.

All The Casualties

From the east, warlords arrive to aid the Millennials. Their crew rises from kneeling, and a resounding roar echoes underwater. The battle ensues as they seize control of weathered seacrafts belonging to fighters and the drug cartel's underdogs. Many perish from mine explosions as the working Wobbaquas escape for their lives. Millennial deploys war wagon buses to rescue them before the cartel strikes.

Amidst the carnage, Aquifers demonstrate their water-based prowess, eliminating most workers and leaving the culprits to be dealt with. Clad in specialized gear, the cartel forces retaliate, but Aquifers execute the specified targets.

The Millennial army stands alongside the frozen Bucklebacks, creating an opening in the dust room wall to release the remaining isopods and free the workers. Cartel-installed individuals inspect the mines but retreat as blasts halt their activities. The war wages on for days, with roaring chariots decimating foot soldiers and dragon-drawn carriages dismantled.

Millennial people engage from a distance, shooting at those who ride to battle in wagons. The conflict culminates in a designated area as a tribute to the fallen, the Wobbaqua Wall of the Dead.

Each family will get one of these with all that information inside.

The Seawall of Names preserves the memory of those who have passed away. Each name magically appears on a water wall in hieroglyphics when the Wobbaquas' life force departs their body. These inscriptions endure throughout the aquatic world, serving as a lasting tribute. It is hoped that no more wars will plague the undersea civilization.
The underwater realm exists in a unique time within a dome-like structure.

A special feature allows the names of the departed to be displayed on the outer surface of the memorial. The Great Dome's wall is situated on the seafloor, and families eagerly come to witness their loved one's name come to life, accompanied by light and a picture of the deceased. This touching display brings solace to the survivors and their families as they cherish the memory of their departed kin.

Chapter Thirteen

Casualties

The war rages on, resembling a man's scorn of imagination, with many bodies as casualties. "Many hang from trees beside the roadways, and many are eaten by water dogs, reaching for what they can reach. Those hanging are eaten from the waist down, while many scraps with one another after the fallen remain, reaching as high as they can. The dogs jump, eating even farther upon the Wobbaqua's body. There seems a place close by had a woman hanging from a tree at one point, as I can remember," Millennial said.

"The place they are hanging resembles how they found her body, as I remember. A man's scorn shows in the scene of the woman's death and how those hang from a noose. The war has taken some of these from their loved ones. You would think someone would come and cut them down to save grace for their families," Millennial said.

"Then war is that way, morbid, and many left to be eaten by buzzards, wild animals on land, underwater animals that keep the deep clean and functioning," the Ol man swore.

Turning slowly to erase this morbid scene from his thoughts and mind, the old soldier steps sideways to a pickup truck bed, slips a sheath and a long knife from his pocket, and slithers the knife through the rope that has seven people hanging beside the roadway on posts.

The seadogs come again and again to feed. The Ol man kicks them away with his pointed steel-toed boots, running them from their feeding grounds.

Standard turns to see an old woman with maggots dripping from her legs; he takes on compassion and asks her, "Why don't you climb into the back of his truck?" She steps in, and then he drives her to the ferry beside the seashore. She steps to the dock and rests her legs under the salty seawater.

The fish are mostly ocean carp, slowly eating the maggots from her legs. She sits for an hour while her legs become clear. It seems the saltwater helps eliminate the pests and the fish eating them.

"Come here," he asked her, returning to stand before him. He wraps her legs with clean gauze and a few strips of surgical tape to let them continue to heal, placing powder into the wound because maggots can't work through powder.

"You do what I have done daily," the Ol man said while chewing on a bone. "You have to come here for three days and let the fish feed to rid yourself of the insects. After three days, if there are any left, you will die or turn into a fly. So, make it a point to do what I ask you!"

The sunset dwindles like a fallen leaf, and the older woman is taken home to rest and heal. Wiping his brow solemnly with his dingy shirt sleeve, the Ol man pressed the knife back into its place, securing his old Sheath of rustic leather. Shaking his head, he wonders about those who live close by and how they could come by here and see this without calling out for help in getting these poor souls down from here, looking at those still hanging from the roped trees.

Looking in the distance as the morning fog has the sunbeams seeping through, the Ol Man sees many homes unaffected by the battle, and he wonders even more about the occupants.

"Are there children in there to cause the family not to want them to see such a thing? There needs to be a squad to get these wounded, stricken, and dead out of existence before children can come upon this scene! Once the stumped bodies fell upon the shell bed beneath the bloody residue, the underlying crustaceans began to move. He remembers that the sea comes alive with Snells eating the meat from the bones of those who have fallen to this sort of death."

Climbing fast into his battered old Chevy pickup truck, he starts the engine as the Snells cover the outside of his truck. Rolling up his windows very quickly, he guns the engine. He moves away from this scene, looking hard into his rearview mirror as the remainder of the bodies are consumed into the ground by the Snells, becoming invisible to the naked eye.

"That could explain why no one took the time to cut the bodies down. In the first place, they were afraid of getting consumed," he said, looking to his right and back at the roadway before him. A sign says, "Do not leave your vehicle in this area! I must have missed that coming in from the other direction, with so many seabirds the Snells have to consume, then return to their Snell beds, because the birds and Snells are a part of the food chain anyway," Robert contends.

Humming, he turns the radio into a concert with the volume so loud and drives on past all this morbidity that has come onto the live scene for him, right in his face. Humming and singing, there in the distance is an Indian reservation of Wobbaquas. "A funny-looking bunch of Wobbaquas to me," he thought. "Different areas house many that think they are another nationality.

Above the ground are many that will be burned ever since the battle left them with many dead Indian Wobbaqua bodies," he explains.

"They have a few isopods placed upon one of the slings they have built to house the dead anyway. So many isopods have them stacked one over the other. War brings many who fall, so many that burial, anyway, it can happen that will work, regretting what is seen as war casualties."

Robert drives into a Sonication drive-in for kelp sandwiches and ocean turnip fries. "Bring me a tall drink to go with that," Robert said. "It's been a long day for me; I hope my old, weak stomach can hold all that," Robert thought, waiting for his order as he watched many vehicles with bodies on them pass the drive-in restaurant.

"Damn, I have carried the thought with me here as they pass by," he thinks. There seems to be a stench in the air of death anyway. Rolling up his truck window to kill the smell, he turns his radio back on. "Sometimes I wonder if the ones on the reservation called Indians have the right idea about life anyway," Robert thought. "So many questions, yet we know the war was a necessity. We, as true Wobbaquas, have to keep the Wobbaqua world clean. Criminals like those who infiltrated the colonies are out as far as Wobbaquas are concerned," Robert said, "without any discomfort on anything that lives beneath the deep." Robert rolls his thoughts.

Outside his driver's side window, there appears a cute little teen, Wobbaqua, to deliver his food. Paying with a small piece of sea glass, he tells her to "keep the change." She takes the money, smiles, and her long Indian face lights up. Bubbles press from his root beer straw as he drinks that first drink. "Whew, refreshing," Robert said while watching the teenie bopper slither back to her post inside a small cavern at the restaurant.

While eating his hamburger of crabmeat and lobster claw, ground ham meat, and fish fries with tardy sauce, Robert sinks into the thought of where he has been and what a magnificent difference he has made in the aquatic world. Coming through the area is the equipment used in the battle, and one thing, he said, that chariot came to the rescue in saving my butt once while fighting. These folks need to be thankful that this old wagon is still running, taking folks back to where they belong.

Chapter Fourteen

Their Need to Rebuild

Many are drawn by the left-behind Wobbaquas that shelter the ocean floor's lining. They transport the exhausted ones to their underwater civilization for safety and happiness, restoring the Wobbaquas world to its accustomed normality. Some are in hospitals, while others retire completely. Happiness returns as manufacturing companies eliminate war debris and restructure to produce goods to sustain the remaining population. "Healthy individuals will propagate new Wobbaquas, replenishing those lost to isopod manufacturing," a Millennial explains. "There might be a minor setback, but the Wobbaquas produce two offspring simultaneously. This will quickly recover our losses."

Hidden from society, they live as they're accustomed to, united and willing to sacrifice for each other. They provide shells and materials to rebuild war-torn areas. Aware of the Wobbaquas' needs, who were once enslaved people to the isopod beds, many underwent counseling to reintegrate into society as productive citizens.

At the peak of the pyramid in the city, upper-class wobbaquas, along with Millennial and orbital men, thrive. They flourish in the deep pyramids and adjacent underwater castles. Smiles brighten the underwater world as the balance is restored. War struck this region, but Millennials are content with the outcome of the war against crime and the return of the isopod beds for food production.

"Freedom isn't free... God bless the soldiers and their families we commemorate today. They are the reason for our existence in the greatest Seaworld in the universe's history. Let's remember on this day who held the line!" Millennial declares.

The isopod beds are restructured, and the deepwater vents are reopened. Sunken ships on the ocean floor provide shelter for feeding fish, and the Wobbaquas use salvaged pieces to craft hand tools for themselves. Meanwhile, the sinking of human life continues toward the depths. Many drown in the struggle to return to sinking ships, grasping for each other. Wobbaquas hear these distressing cries through the seawater. Seaworthy vessels and underwater crafts guide the human race to their familiar environment. The wobbaquas are placed back into their world to be forgotten by humans.

Brick Thunder and Millennial men return to their respective domains, each fulfilling their purpose of maintaining peace in a well-functioning society.

Many ventures to the isopod farmlands, working to restore the landmasses and produce enough food for the Wobbaqua civilization before hurricane season or a volcanic eruption disrupts their efforts. Animal feces are used as fertilizer, and some former field workers have stopped since acquiring wealth. "Once they find the shelves empty and the streets crumbling, they'll reconsider contributing to this free society," Millennial remarks. "Ultimately, they'll quiet their hungry stomachs or evade a shark's bite!" His voice carries years of wisdom.

Chapter Fifteen

Closing Back into The Deep

Ascending above the serene ocean surface, the expansive dome with its massive circumference was elevated. An array of Aquifers was brought up to the surface through an astronomical magnetic air force, one with the potential to disrupt the Earth's axis. Gracefully cradling the water, the dome floated like a silky au jus gravy drizzled over a steak.

The Millennial man stood atop the central peak of the rounded glass dome structure, accompanied by his brother's counterpart. Together, they observed the sun descending, casting an orange and lavender hue upon the water world's ruggedness. The encompassing domes veiled a sense of gloominess. Side by side, they awaited the return of the celestial spacecraft that had transported them to this abyssal aquatic realm. Millennial and Orbital stood united, sharing a profound inner affection. As the sunset gradually transformed into a reddish lavender glow, it spread its luminance across the expanse of the oceanic waters.

As darkness falls, the domes are gently lowered back into their designated positions, assuming their dormant state, much like they have for countless millennia. This action marks the conclusion of yet another chapter in the lives of Millennial and Orbital men. Only one is turned over among the domes, a task mastered by the old mechanic in the aircraft hangar.

With the completion of these tasks, Millennial embarks on a journey across the continent, departing from the shores of Mexico. Beneath the waters of the Pacific Ocean lies the submerged city of Philiffi, a sister city where Millennial resides. An intricately crafted collection of statues beautifully embellishes the city's entrance. Upon Millennial's arrival and as he stands before the opening of Philippi, his presence is magical, as he is here to perform a singular task: to reawaken the city to live.

Drawing upon his vast intelligence and memory bank, Millennial contemplates, "We may have been nourished by Dragon milk, but we are purebred Wobbaquas." These words resonate as he gazes at the statuesque soldiers standing guard beside the Hudson River on the outskirts of New York City. His memory takes him back, and he recalls that these soldiers were once living beings. Turning his attention to the nearby island, another statue comes to life. Then, he shifts his gaze to the opposite island, where yet another statue springs to life. Although situated beneath the ocean's depths, these beings can respire underwater, sustained until the Millennial fulfills his purpose.

Proceeding into the city, he sends lightning bolts in all directions, followed by a concentrated surge through the waters. The city begins its majestic ascent from the seabed floor, where it has rested for centuries. Notably, the vents responsible for providing oxygenated water to the city inhabitants have a significant opening just before the city's entrance. Water cascades from its structure as the city rises, gracefully transitioning from submerged to suspended mid-water, gradually emerging above the ocean's surface.

Resting there for three days, the city soaks under the intense Pacific sun, with barnacles and plankton growth accumulated over the years baking and crumbling away. After this rejuvenation, the city is lowered back to its habitable depths, ready for Wobbaquas to establish homes for themselves and their families. Priority is given to those suffering from the drug war, especially the vulnerable ones. Compassion for fellow Wobbaquas takes precedence.

Each family is entrusted with planting trees, symbolizing their growth, finances, and overall happiness. A stern rule is established by a father, declaring that it will be felled if the family's finances fail to thrive along with the tree. The family will regress to indulgent self-pity, wallowing in their misfortunes. This underscores the Wobbaqua values of growth, family prosperity, and personal responsibility.

Yet, some Wobbaquas succumb to self-pity, contrasting the true Wobbaqua essence. It measures their dedication to family growth, happiness, and finances. Support from fellow Wobbaquas is not automatic; individuals must strive to better their circumstances. Millennial emphasizes this perspective, stating that those who fail to nurture their tree and finances show apathy, a sign they should return to their origins.

Having concluded his efforts, Millennial returns to his beloved, waiting at the pyramid's base. His thoughts turn to his impending union with her, a love unlike any he's experienced before. She understands his love, and he cherishes her deeply. As they prepare to wed, there's a pressing concern – a looming threat to the sea that the Wobbaquas must address.

The Wobbaqua tradition of marrying beyond their species incurs the Father's displeasure, but the Millennial waits for his blessings. Ultimately, the Father conveys his approval telepathically, bringing tears to Millennial's eyes. The Father reveals that the chosen bride will become queen and commends the Millennial's understanding of the complex situation.

Millennial embraces his mission with the Father's blessing and vows to return after sharing the news with his future wife. Crossing the divide to reach the landmass, he hears her voice resonating across the sea's surface.

Standing before her, they share a heartfelt embrace, and he relays the Father's approval. Marlina, growing accustomed to his aquatic appearance, expresses her profound love.

In this intricate world of aquatic beings, the bonds of love, duty, and responsibility intertwine, creating a tapestry of emotions and actions that shape the destiny of the Wobbaqua civilization.

Placing a kiss on his lips, Marlina smiles. He kisses her back ever so softly with a deep, burning passion. With each kiss, their souls intertwine in emotions. Suddenly pulling from one another, they realize they must wait for the concentration of the wedding vows. Stepping holding hands, they whisper to one another and giggle.

"I have wedding advisors ready to plan our wedding." Marlina

"Especially since I saw how you reacted to the emotional spin of seeing the gown and everything," Millennial said.

Stepping to the park bench, Millennial speaks of the wedding inside the domes.

"I love your ideas," Marlina said.

"We can plan on using the main dome area; it is massive and will seat a thousand at least?"

"The grandeur of the wedding will be written into the history books of the underworld for a millennial."

"The tables and all the decorations will be taken care of. We have to decide; what flowers do we want to use?"

"What is your favorite flower, Marlina?" Millennial asked.

"Roses!" "I love white roses, maybe a little pink and some blue."

"What kind do you like?" "Any kind is good with me," Millennial said, giggling.

"That settles it, my love. We will have the biggest wedding in the underworld of the sea abyss."

"The melodious band will play your selection for our dance."

The table covers will be a soft yellow color with the greenery of eucalyptus and roses. Additionally, with some seagrass draping onto the tablecloth, softened by some pale green ribbon accents."

This may change before the wedding." Transforming into a man when the kiss is on his lips.

"When are we saying our vows?" Marlina asked.

"One month from today," Millennial said. "

"I must return to the deep now and finalize the planning. Therefore, we will be having the wedding."

Stepping away from Marlina, she released her hand while letting her hand drop to her side. Returning to the plantation, she waits.

"I must go." Stepping into his transformation into a millennial seaman. He metamorphoses while he sinks beneath the depths. Traveling to the outskirts of Phallifi, the city of the Gods! Taking care of the business there, he heads back home to help Marlina plan the wedding.

The Wobbaquas pass a band of frog giggers beside the roadway. They are doing a three-frog jam session, playing "Welcome to The Underwater Jungle," and spouting out the *ddi, dd, d d* loudly. Smiling at their happiness, he swims on into the gated pyramids. Traveling to his private dome. Inside to his bed where he rests lightly. Realizing he will be making a change for the better. Refreshing the usual lifestyle, he has known for Millennials time.

"I have to have someone in my life right now!" He thinks while rolling into his mesh silver bed covers with a cooling effect. Looking at the wall. He sets his eyes on an original Picasso painting. At the same time, he wondered about his fate in life. Besides, he left many pieces of art for people to gaze at. "Wonder how motion works as a quiver," he said; he fell fast to sleep.

"The moon and the galaxy There in the night sky. The ocean opens its belly, letting the Millennial star watch till he is fast asleep. "This is my home of homes. I live by the rules of the universe. My born home in the depths has been sufficient. I have lived to conquer the deep. I have a woman I love.

My cup runneth over. Sometimes, I stir my coffee with a bent spoon handle."

Practically digging the bottom out of the cup.

"I promise to lighten up my emotions," Millennial said.

"My world is complete. Now that I have found true love for another. Although human, she can exist in my world. With the transformation of I in hers. The wealth of the world is before us. Being an aquifer myself. There will be no more hunger in the upper world as we implement the harvests of food grown in the depths. Two worlds intertwined for the benefit of life in both worlds!"

Chapter Sixteen
Return to the Depths

Returning his true love to the lengthy pier that stretches along the land behind her house, overlooking the expanse of the oceanic view, Marina halts to reverse her sprint into his embrace. She pauses as he slips into the water, aware that she will serenade her heart out for his nightly return. A truer love has never existed like the one she shares with Millennial men.

Swiftly swimming at the speed of sound, he arrives at the city walls. Opening the gates, he catches the sun's rays dancing off the domes. He navigates towards the cliff above the city, a gesture of peace as a group of herrings arrives to deliver the sunshine. Their scales reflect and amplify the brightness before his eyes.

Standing with his arms outstretched, he recites a poem about the right to freedom in the world he oversees.

How majestic is thy grandeur,
How marvelous your inhabitants,
Oh! How taken, I am at such excellence in the creation,
My heart sings of your makings,
The beauty inside, All the inhabitants reside,
This alone, the father takes pride in,
A desert of love hides inside,
May we stand for one and be by each other's side,
Oh! The love we share in an oceanic pride,
We stand as one Wobbaqua and have nothing to hide,
The secrets of the underworld are where we reside.
Coming together, you as my beautiful bride,
Both coincide with loving as one without unjust pride,

May a millennial come as we grow as one
leaving our feelings of lust aside,
Man and wife, the aquatic world is our footstool
the upper world out of control
That left to the fool. Some untold.
You're the reason I exist. Oh, my soul.

The Wedding of Royalty

Drowning in invitations and clutter from the opened packages sent to the plantation, Marlina readies herself to plan her wedding with the Millennials. She opens a can of "la leche" milk and spoons a bowl of Salt-o-meal, sipping her coffee in between. Upon closer inspection, she realizes she'll need to outsource some tasks that will consume time.

"I'll enlist an agency to handle the invitation mailings," she decides. "The services of a florist can adorn the dome rooms, and many Wobbaquas can offer their assistance, too. My Millennial partner will take care of all these details, especially since our wedding will be in the depths," Marlina asserts, referring to the underwater world of the Wobbaquas.

We crafted seashell vases for the flowers and fashioned table runners from burlap seaweed. "I adore orchestrating all of this," she mused. With a graceful swish of his hand, the room burst into illumination. The shimmer of electric eels cast light on each table. A surge of blue electrical current ran through the table covers, enhancing the flowers as if by magic. The room and its decorations transformed into a spectacle of grandeur, unfolding right before Marina's eyes.

In awe, she turned toward the Millennial man and embraced him tightly. Marina appeared bright-eyed and capable, radiating vivacity and a distinctive narrative. Her beauty and good humor had drawn the Millennials closer to marriage. Sensing her emotions, he yearned for more than just a hug from her. He desired to spend every moment of his time with her.

"The dome above their heads takes on an elevated appearance. The very foundation of the expansive room appears to shift upward. As they stood on it, the floor underwent resurfacing. The walkways leading to the wedding chamber are swiftly redone. Everything transforms into a brilliant cream hue. The lighting switches to L.E.D!!! This accentuates those inside, causing them to radiate more brightly, with the true luster of Millennial scales coming to light," the family exclaimed.

The Wedding Preparation

The staff is uniformed to cater to the guests, each server having undergone proper training for this consistent type of service. The tables are filled with carefully prepared and monumental dishes, ready to satisfy both those from the upper world and those from the sea.

The wedding day draws nearer, and all the workers gather to adorn the room. The surrounding area has expanded to a massive scale, revealing breathtaking beauty. Within the bride's quarters hangs a diamond-laced white wedding dress embellished with shimmering sea glass of various colors around the neckline. Specifically, chosen magic strings adorn the intricately woven fabric, with silver accents woven into the threads. The length of the train is designed to suit the size of the room where the ceremony will take place.

Her veil, made of fine satin edged with Malay, matches the length of the train and is adorned with chiffon and diamonds across her headdress. These elements are intricately interwoven throughout the fabric, extending gracefully to the floor and embellishing the sparkling diamond clusters. The bride's shoes are made of shale and a cream oyster-colored pump. The soles are adorned with delicate stones, and pearls line the sides of the shoes, with natural seawater pearls precisely inlaid on the toe. The wedding gown will glide smoothly across these top decorations, while the sides of the soles and heels are also studded with diamonds. The strap is a wrap-around style, featuring a large quarter-sized pearl around the ankle.

She wears a shoe with a slip-through hole, securing it with an ankle latch. Her arms are adorned with lace-lined chiffon gloves, and the finest quality stones are intertwined in the mesh. The woven fabric showcases a Spanish lace design. Around the waist of her wedding gown lies an embedded pearl and diamond sash, tying in the front and draping gracefully to the floor.

The white hue in her clothing is pristine, catching her eye as it hangs on a hook. This exquisite attire captivates her attention as she wanders from one chamber to another. Marina finds herself drifting back into the bride's chamber, where she can't help but admire the beauty of her gown and accessories.

She will wear a necklace of square diamonds around her neck, channel set into white gold, each set of the highest quality. Sliding her hand across the glass case that houses this exquisite piece of jewelry, a tear escapes her eye. She steps into the foyer to return to where Millennial is and reaches out to him.

"I sensed your tears falling to the floor, my love," Millennial softly speaks. Emerging from the groom's chambers, he spots Marlina standing in the hallway. After ensuring his Sharkskin suit, cummerbund, tie, shoes, and the wedding ring on a small pillow are all in place, he gazes at Marlina.

"I apologize, my love. I'm utterly amazed by all this beauty," Marina admits.

"Come, let's take you back home. You appear exhausted to me," Millennial suggests, encasing Marlina in an air bubble.

"Our wedding day will arrive soon enough."

Taking Marlina by the arm, he guides her to a waiting limousine, his beckoning drawing her outside. "Come close to me, my love," Millennial invites, sliding his arm around Marlina as they embrace, wrapped in affection.

Meanwhile, the driver navigates the rough terrain, causing discomfort that Millennial senses through Marlina. Utilizing their telepathic connection, he propels the limousine through the water like a predestined, fueled rocket. Suddenly, the wheels retract beneath the car's body, transforming it into a vehicle gliding through the water with the sensation of floating at high speed.

Amidst this journey, they exchange emotions, marking a significant breakthrough in their relationship. Their empathic connection allows him to feel her emotions, and she reciprocates, creating an intimate exchange. As their emotions soar, they become enveloped in the limousine, their feelings intensifying like an electric shock between their bodies, leading to a pulsating connection.

Chapter Seventeen
The Proposal

"Wow, Marlina, this is an unfamiliar experience for me," Millennial said.

"Me too," Marlina raised her voice as we covered her clothing with a gentle blue flame. They are so naive about their physical makeup and don't understand these feelings. They are like fresh cuts of fabric. Nevertheless, they wallow in the instinct to repeat this behavior.

"This has to happen again, Marlina," Millennial said excitedly. Millennial's soul spot glowed in the darkness of the depths while he returned to his usual strict demeanor and posture. "I agree, Millennial."

"I've never felt anything like that before."

"We are almost home, approaching the entrance to the city. Straighten yourself before we arrive, my love."

"I'm anxious for you to see my living quarters and how we exist in the depths," he spoke telepathically through the water, directly addressing the one he loves so deeply. With her heart beating in her ears, she held the hand of the man she loved so deeply, even though all she could see was water for a long time. Marlina held on tightly.

Suddenly, a reflection spiraled—a sparkling sea glass dome appeared so magnificent before them. The massive gateway came into existence. She was in awe of such a structure with its golden hues, a dome of such magnitude.

Swimming beside Millennial, she watched as he placed an invisible dome over her head to protect her eyes from the pressure change when they ventured into the void of the seawater and then into the air-filled room. He was capable of the transformation, but her eyes were sensitive. He knew this and was making her as comfortable as possible.

Looking around, she saw this new world, so different from the one she was born into. Her face was still flushed from the transformation she had undergone.

"It's from the excitement of being with you, Millennial," she said.

"I know. While I was in the bride and groom chamber, entering this magical world as we did is incredibly intriguing," she added, her thoughts lingering on the recent sensual encounter they had shared.

"I understand, my love," Millennial reassured her. "We'll complete all our tasks to move forward with our lives. These encounters will become a daily occurrence."

"Remember the plan, and you'll do just fine. Stay focused," he advised.

"Once we adhere to the societal rules and formalize our mar riage with words and actions, only then can we truly do as we please," Millennial explained.

Marlina composed herself as a Millennial prepared to return to the depths. He remained in the limousine seat, thinking about their recent encounter. "This woman just rocked my world," he thought, contemplating how it took a long time to catch up on things left behind.

Upon arriving at the domes, he stepped out of the limousine and into his watery world. The sensation of seawater on his skin felt refreshing, akin to a shower after a long rush. He stood by, waiting for the city gate to open and admit him.

As the aquatic gate's clock began to close, signaling the end of this day's activities, guards arrived to escort him beneath the dome structure and guide his path through the depths. Lying in the stillness of his resting place, Millennial's mind wandered to his true love. Immersed in his emotions, he drifted into a deep slumber, only to be awakened by a light beam. Reality snapped back, and he mentally noted the tasks for the upcoming day, particularly the imminent wedding. He checked in with Orbital, his wedding coordinator, and contacted his brother. Meanwhile, the morning was breaking at Marlina's palace. Millennial called out to his brother.

"Do you have everything in order, Orbital?" Millennial inquired.

"Yes, I do. You know my daily routine," Orbital responded, speaking from across the room as he transitioned into the water in his room. The scene showed Orbital carrying out his routine while conversing with his brother. Both of them were multitasking and engaged in their daily activities. Zooming in midair helped convey the timeframe.

"That's great!"

"Now, this new life adventure will help bridge the gap between humans and Wobbaquas."

"Be careful, my brother. With just one mistake, you could destroy the universe!" Orbital scolded.

"I know, I know. I'm treading on thin water," Millennial admitted.

"I had an experience I want to share with you."

"Maybe you can remind me when we're not zooming, Orbital? I'll tell you about my ride in a limousine!" Millennial suggested.

"What was it, Millennial?" Orbital asked, suspended in mid-air. "Oh, my brother! I'd rather tell you in person! A hint? Can I get a hint?" Orbital inquired.

Millennial spoke softly at first, then his voice erupted with emotion. "The love of my life allowed me to feel her emotions during a sensual encounter."

"A human's feelings are different from a Wobbaquas."

"We shared a mixture of our emotions. It wasn't just a physical contact thing. I felt like I was taken away from my existence while in her embrace," Millennial explained. Orbital stared at his brother's statement in amazement.

"Keep that to yourself. We'll examine that later," Orbital advised, raising his brow. "Hmm?"

"I have to continue with my day."

"We should meet for a drink soon," Orbital suggested, closing the Zoom meeting. Millennial felt refreshed and ready for his wedding day. The servants of a king arrived to escort him.

"We are here to prepare you, Your Majesty!"

Millennial stood ready to don his attire, which was to be arranged to match all the things Marlina had requested for him to wear. He remembered his role as a king, understanding that he needed to address the various issues the monarchy had in store for them. Walking through a small door to his dressing room, he checked his cummerbund, shirt, and tie – all carefully chosen to match each other.

"Everything is acceptable," he said, leaving the dome and venturing into the depths. He had a few matters to attend to, one of which concerned the food supply for the Wobbaqua world. Upon reaching the posting station, he noticed several workers who had previously toiled in the mines.

"Why are they here right now?" he wondered. "Were they released for a specific reason to aid our food supply?"

The old colored Wobbaqua at the weigh-in station flipped open his clipboard, checking the status of a particular Wobbaqua. "Sir, I can confirm that he was cleared by the court to work in the food beds."

"Ensure you verify the status of all those coming to work," Millennial instructed. "Check them based on their court-ordered appearance status."

"That's what happened in the mines. They allowed a few individuals who intended to produce the drug to blend in with the masses and cause an infection."

"We will not tolerate any such foolishness again. Anyone attempting to betray the Wobbaqua world will face execution," he declared sternly.

Millennials swam inside to assess all the workers, many of whom were still frail from their time in the mines. "Their willingness to help the common masses is commendable. However, Wobbaquas must be held accountable to prevent any harm through the food supply," Millennial emphasized. Satisfied with his inspection, he moved on to the bosses in the food fields.

Swimming outside the food domes, Millennial blew his nose – he was allergic to the insecticides used to keep the fields free of water insects. Many of these insects clung to the leaves of plants, weighing them down, he realized. Using fresh kelp from the seabed to wipe his nose, he visited each dome, ensuring that each task was completed before concluding his workday.

Chapter Eighteen

The City Awaits Its Queen

As he swam back to the city, he looked up and noticed the chapel above the domes where the entrance to the pyramid for the wedding was located. The streets were adorned with grand decorations in preparation for the ceremony. The view of the city and its festive atmosphere could be seen through the dome from above.

"I had underestimated the significance of this step,"

Millennial muttered to himself, "I'm unexpectedly bringing a human into our world. I underestimated the significance of this step."

"I assume the Wobbaqua world has accepted her arrival?" he questioned inwardly.

"We can only hope that an offspring from us will possess Wobbaqua traits," Millennial pondered, his thoughts drifting to the future. He readied himself for the pampering that would precede the upcoming ceremony. Returning to the palace, he washed off the seawater, ate a few bites, and then settled down for a brief rest. The anticipation of reuniting with his lifelong love kept him excited.

As the new day dawned, the wedding bells echoed throughout the city. Millennial arose, feeling refreshed. He prepared to adorn his lapel with a crown and the finest jewels.

"Dressed as a king, Marlina will be surprised," he mused. "So will her family. Once my world recognizes me as the 'King Wobbaqua,' I'll assume human form." Millennial inserted his desires into the plan, asserting his authority, saying, "I'm the king, and my way is the only way!"

With meticulous planning, the wedding coordinator left Millennial's presence, escorted by security. Other Wobbaqua workers meticulously handled the remaining details.

"The bridal march will be to the new queen's choice. King Millennial's walk will follow her lead as well," the wedding coordinator informed.

Nerves were taut as the long day wore on. The pyramid's entrance opened into the watery expanse. Many guests chose to enclose themselves in personal seawater domes. This option accommodated those who found it easier to breathe underwater.

Lines of Wobbaquas eagerly awaited the wedding procession. Outside the palace, people mingled in anticipation of the royal wedding, an opulent event unfolding beneath the sea.

"It's going to be an unforgettable event in the underwater world," a reporter commented.

Around 600,000 individuals gathered in the streets, awaiting the start of the century's grandest wedding.

Marlina had chosen the sparkling ring she planned to wear, now adorning her finger. However, controversy surrounded her choice since the ring originated from a mine deep in the abyss. It was believed that only the wealthiest could afford such a jewel. The palace was less than thrilled with this decision, preferring a more traditional choice. Despite its size, Marlina intended to make the diamond ring fit her hand over time, ensuring it would suffice for the wedding.

The wedding was expected to be spectacular, planned entirely by the couple. With a guest list of 3,500 for the pyramid's interior, the grand pyramid's hallway was enlisted to accommodate the crowd, leading to the ceremony's ballroom in the Grand Hall. Although there were some objections due to the guest list cuts, Marlina and King Millennial remained steadfast in their plans.

One captivating aspect of the royal wedding was that, for the first time in over 3000 years, a "commoner" was marrying the heir to the Wobbaqua throne. The wedding was grand, lavish, and unprecedented in scale. Considering the numerous guests and the substantial security required to protect the couple and attendees, the event cost was estimated to be around $48 million in world dollars, though that figure might still be underestimated. Meanwhile, the Father eagerly awaited the opportunity to convey the wedding news to the royals in a world far across space within the universe of the great Wobbaqua realm.

"With over 5,000 police officers of the Wobbaqua army deployed for crowd control, the event is well managed. After all, 600,000 attendees are lining the streets along the couple's two-mile route outside the pyramid structure," the security team reported.

Marlina's gown was nothing short of spectacular, designed by a group of Wobbaquas who understood the taste of their king. One of the designers shared, "We aimed for drama, a portrayal of everyone's fairy princess fantasy. The timing was perfect for that, embracing frills and ruffles."

"Though it's heartbreaking, she will be the reigning queen until her passing, as Millennial possesses the secret to longevity," others acknowledged. "As difficult as it is, he will marry and have multiple wives. However, she is special because she is the first to teach him how to be a husband," some speculated about the significance of the union.

Chapter Nineteen

The Wedding Day

Bringing their families together, they used the past war's leftover submarines. Each city portal had doors leading into the main pyramid, where the wedding ceremony would take place. Small rooms were available for changing, offering privacy for each family to prepare. As they waited for the ceremony to commence, they were awestruck by the grand sight of the domes from the depths of the sea.

Whales and sharks swam gracefully in the vicinity as the sea life had become accustomed to the presence of the domes. The airflow within the domes created a cool temperature outside the glass structure. Those from Marlina's family were comfortably situated within the oxygenated domes, specially designed for human guests since their arrival.

All the wedding preparations had been meticulously attended to. Millennials commented, "Such a wedding is a once-in-a-lifetime affair."

Throughout the morning, all attendees gathered at the opening of the great hall, each holding sealed and wax-stamped invitations that had been cleared through security. The family members were placed at the back of the great hall, conveniently close to the dressing rooms. Light snacks were provided to them in small quantities, as a grand reception meal was planned after the wedding ceremony.

The archways had been meticulously decorated by individuals chosen specifically for the task. Cream-colored water lilies, seagrass, and cattails adorned the arch, set against a backdrop of sparkling sea glass and burlap. The effect was breathtakingly elegant. The tables and candelabras were similarly adorned, following the same color scheme. Tall silver trellises graced the center of each table, adorned with white water lilies, spring ariah, and cascading wedding bell flowers. The room was filled with the delightful aroma of gardenias, creating a magnificent display fit for royalty.

Each table was set with cream colored Satinique fabric and a full-place setting. The crystal goblets gleamed in the light, a testament to their exquisite quality. Cream Satinique fabric covered the long tables, accented with strips of burlap and an array of flowers, including Dindorodian orchids, wedding bells, and sea moss. Diamond-toned sparkling sea glass added accents to the arrangements. The teardrop crystal glass chandeliers were lowered to become part of the decorations, adding a touch of elegance to the scene.

The moment had arrived. Marlinas' hand was placed in Millennial's as he led her to the altar, where the priest of the sea would administer their vows. The room was grand, allowing for a lengthy train on the bride's dress. With Marlinas now standing by his side, Millennial stepped away, sitting beside the bride's mother with tears in his eyes as he awaited the ceremony.

As the bride took her place to the left side, next to the ring bearer, a hushed silence fell over the room, anticipatory and filled with excitement for the upcoming ceremony. The attendees couldn't help but express awe as they entered the room and beheld the breathtaking setup. The bride's father, filled with emotion, inquired, his voice quivering with pride and love.

"What have we gotten ourselves into now?" Marlinas' mother's voice trembled with emotion. "Is this what our grandchildren will look like?" Her tears flowed uncontrollably, reflecting her mix of emotions.

"Be still, my love. There must be a good ending to all of this. If Marlina has chosen a man of this stature, we must accept it as she does. She is in love," Marlinas' father tried to console her.

"The room is filled with people, and the silence returns," Marlinas' father continued, attempting to soothe his wife's distress.

As the pastor-clergy entered the room, a sense of solemnity settled in. Then, the bridal march song, chosen by Millennials, began to play, performed by the corner orchestra. The groom and his father appeared, dressed for the occasion. The wedding procession had lined up at the back of the grand hall.

A chorus of "awws" filled the room as guests entered, awed by the magnificence of the space and its decorations. Across the room, the bride's family members noticed many individuals who had not yet undergone the transformation to human standards. The shock was evident on their faces as they witnessed the appearance of humans who did not resemble them. Each guest was designated to enter when their turn in the wedding procession arrived.

Chapter Twenty

The Ceremony

The pastor took his place behind the archway, and soft music began to play, signaling the families to enter and take their seats. Bridesmaids and groomsmen followed suit, with the ring bearer entering alongside the bridesmaids. The flower girl gracefully dribbled rose petals along the aisle as she made her way. Distraught yet determined, Marlinas' father stepped into a side door momentarily and rejoined the procession. Waiting in the hallway outside the great hall, he watched as children resembling the bride dropped rose petals onto the aisle while the crowd eagerly anticipated the bride's entrance.

Marlina's stunning appearance left her father emotional and questioning. "What have we done? Is this what our grandchildren will look like?" he asked, his voice full of concern. Her mother, stifling her anguish, responded, "Be still, my love. There must be meaning in all this. If Marlina has chosen a man of this stature, we must accept it." She added, "She loves him," with a sigh.

Amid the anticipation, the groomsmen entered the room, taking their places beside the groom. The bridesmaids followed, each wearing beautiful beige and cream-colored satin dresses. Floor-length gowns with draped sea moss and spring ayah carried small bouquets adorned with a few white baby roses.

The wedding dress was a marvel, adorned with diamond baguettes along the sweeping hemline. The off-shoulder design featured intricate details like a mesh fabric intertwined with emerald-hued elements.

She wore shoes overlaid with sea-green kelp and transparent fabric, accented with pearls. As Marlina stood next to the king, she felt a comforting breeze envelop her, thanks to the dome of air he had placed around everyone who needed it.

The vows were spoken, the promise of fidelity emphasized by the pastor. "You may kiss your bride!" With those words, Marlena and Millennial shared a passionate kiss, their emotions intertwined. Their connection was profound—she saw him as a human, the man she fell in love with, and he saw her as the same.

Hand in hand, they left the wedding area, photographers documenting their departure. Every aspect of the ceremony was revered, a sacred event deserving respect from all in attendance.

The strains of the bridal march echoed loudly, reaching the underwater city through the walls of the magnificent pyramid. Mermaids and aquatic creatures gathered at the dome in the seawater, eagerly watching the wedding procession unfold with excitement and joy.

The door swung open, revealing Marlina in her exquisitely designed gown. Her veil gently draped over her face, clasping her father's arm. The bridesmaids meticulously adjusted her train, ensuring that the elegant stones sewn into the fabric displayed their brilliance as planned.

Marlina completed her bridal march toward the altar, stepping gracefully on the rose and multicolored dendroidal orchid petals scattered by sea children. Her radiance brought a smile to Millennial's face, who was delighted by her beauty. He sensed her anticipation through their soul connection, and his excitement overflowed.

As the children retreated from the procession, Marlina stood before her groom. Her eyes sparkled, and Millennial felt her heart devotedly belonging to him. He knew his life would be infinitely enriched by her presence, solely his throughout her lifetime.

They turned their attention to the minister, a man of indistinct ethnicity but profound wisdom. Marlina's smile was hidden beneath her veil, and as they reached for each other, she delicately brushed the veil aside, revealing her face. Millennial was struck still by her polished elegance, his breath momentarily taken away.

He took her hand, and the minister, perceptive to Millennial's emotions, continued the ceremony befitting their royal status. The wedding vows were spoken slowly, their promises binding them together.

Millennial accepted the ring from the young bearer and placed it on Marlina's finger. Their connection deepened as she felt his gratitude through their bond. Taking the next ring, Marlina placed it on Millennial's finger. The minister delivered a sermon on values, concluding with the phrase, "You may now kiss your bride." Millennials drew closer; their lips kissed gently, symbolizing their unity.

The minister directed them to take their first steps as a married couple, and they gracefully descended from the podium, heading towards the door of the grand chapel. A magnificent carriage awaited them, drawn by two massive seahorses. The harnesses were adorned with precious stones from the sea beds, diamonds, and rubies woven into the intricate design. As they marveled at the sight, Millennial assured Marlina, "Only the finest for royalty, and you are royalty now."

Though the Galaxy's *'Paranites'* might disagree with their unconventional union, Millennial understood that this life, predestined by external forces, held no value without the love they shared. As they soared through the skies of the upper world, invisible and unheard, he reflected, "They seeded this planet with the Wobbaquas. Now, they must let us decide what is best for our world."

The wedding procession gathered for dinner after the ceremony, and photographers captured the precious moments. Millennial and Marlina entered the magnificent carriage, waving to the onlookers as they were driven to the back of the palace and the pyramid. Returning to the great hall, they joined the massive dinner planned for the occasion.

As they navigated the secret passageways of the pyramid, they entered the grand dining room through a mirror, a touch of enchantment adding to the day's magic. Millennial and Marlina stood side by side, the depth of their love evident to all who beheld them. Though Marlina's time on Earth would be limited, Millennial intended to make every moment unforgettable. As a Wobbaqua, he would live on eternally, cherishing their love through the ages.

They dive into the depths and concentrate on the vows with an underwater kiss.

Their love is consecrated together; they delve deep into the love they share.

Harmonizing both worlds, the two leaders return to their corners of the world.

Millennial wonders about his life as a Wobbaqua. Should Marlina age out from his longevity? Brick Thunder wonders about his life without the precinct daily. Both worlds were in harmony. The leaders were relieved at the outcome. Life goes on.

Set before the king and queen and Orbital at the throne.

Made in United States
North Haven, CT
04 November 2026

21753012R00119